CIRCLE WITHOUT END

For the fires grow cold and the dances fail,
And the songs in their echoes die;
And what have we left but the graves beneath,
And, above, the waiting sky?

Song of the Ancient Ones

CIRCLE WITHOUT END

A Sourcebook of American Indian Ethics

Frances G. Lombardi
Gerald Scott Lombardi

Naturegraph

Library of Congress Cataloging in Publication Data

Circle without end.

   Bibliography: p.
   Includes index.
     1. Indians of North America—Ethics—Addresses,
essays, lectures. 2. Indians of North America—
Philosophy—Addresses, essays, lectures.
I. Lombardi, Frances G., 1925-   II. Lombardi,
Gerald Scott, 1952-
E98.E83C57   1982   170'.8997   82-12481
ISBN 0-87961-114-6
ISBN 0-87961-115-4 (pbk.)

Naturegraph Publishers, Inc.
   P. O. Box 1075
   Happy Camp, CA 96039

Copyright Permissions and Acknowledgments

(The copyright notices listed below and on pages 186-189 constitute
an extension of this copyright page.)

FOOTNOTE 1. "This Newly Created World" is taken from the Winnebago
Medicine Rite as recorded in Paul Radin, *The Road of Life and Death: A Ritual
Drama of the American Indians* (p. 254), Bollingen Series V, copyright 1945 by
Princeton University Press, copyright © renewed 1972 by Princeton University
Press. Reprinted by permission.

FOOTNOTES 2, 7, 19, 24 185. From *The Sacred Pipe: Black Elk's Account of
the Seven Rites of the Oglala Sioux* by Joseph E. Brown. Copyright © 1953 by
University of Oklahoma Press. Reprinted by permission of University of Oklahoma Press.

To AJL whose power was love

Acknowledgment

We are most grateful to those patient native Americans who willingly shared their customs, philosophy, and spiritual legacy with the strangers in their midst. Much is owed to early chroniclers for preserving the history of native Americans in the white man's language. We appreciate the opportunity to mingle our thoughts with theirs.

Denese N. Lombardi and Domingos Lobo are remembered for their encouragement and assistance in assembling bibliographical data.

Gratitude is also due the librarians at Harvard University, the Library of Congress, New Haven Free Public Library, Southern Connecticut State College, the University of New Haven and Yale University, for their cooperation in obtaining source materials. To these tireless and dedicated guardians of the written word, we express in this way, our sincere acknowledgments for their many kindnesses.

Throughout this writing project, we relied daily on our own spirit guide, St. Christopher, for inspiration and fortitude. We, hereby, honor his spiritual presence.

Contents

Preface

The history of human experience is a never-ending spectacle of the people's attempt to cope with their society, ideas, emotions and environment; it is most interesting when presented in the words of those who lived it. The people's reactions to events that shaped their destiny often disclose a comprehension of enduring values and practical wisdom which, in both their conscious and unconscious aspects, formed the principles that governed their lives.

Native American philosophy, not in spite of its ancient origin but because of its antiquity, is a relevant alternative to present-day humanity's self-created image of materialism, artificial posturing, and ethnic conflicts. Native American philosophy is worth examining in terms of modern expectations.

This anthology expresses native Americans' philosophy in their own words, as they experienced it, in a revelation of their humor, their yearning for peace and understanding, their wisdom, pride, and dignity. It fills us with a desire to reach out, to touch the genius of their wisdom, and to feel once more the satisfying pleasure of humankind in a co-partnership with the cosmos.

Our commentaries are not intended to "interpret" native American philosophy, but rather to acknowledge its value in contributing to the people's remarkable moral virtues, family and community life, tribal cohesiveness, courage, and the spiritual strength to endure extremely adverse social and economic afflictions resulting from white monopoly of power. The biographical sketches included in this book offer another view of the people's application of these principles to their personal habits, relationships with others, their ceremonies and the extent to which the people relied on them. The philosophy which sustained native Americans in their dilemma is a viable option to the current mood of uncertainty.

Society is rapidly deteriorating and unable to correlate its beliefs with its behavior, thereby causing a moral crisis in the search for solutions to spiritual, social, political, and environmental problems.

Some indefinable remnant of ancient man resides in us still and nags at our conscience like a shadow. After centuries of neglect, man has begun to listen to these stirrings within himself, and to instinctively surmise that the message and his survival lie in his own nature. Native American time-proven traditions define an intense discovery of the relationship between man and nature in a holy alliance with the Creator. Like a mandala, the unseen essence was a constant presence in their lives.

The Iroquois called it Orenda; the Pawnee thought of it as Tirawa; the Omaha addressed their prayers and thoughts to Wakonda; the Algonquians said it was Manitou; the Sioux whispered it with reverence and named it Wakan-Tanka. They recognized the all-permeating life-force as a gentle spirit of the winds and heavens and the earth and mountains, never tiring of expressing in song and poetry genuine affection for the mystery and magnificence of the ever-changing moods of nature in which native Americans found an inexhaustible joy that touched their innermost being.

We could not refrain from wondering what might have been the destiny of this country and its visionary people had the European intrusion resulted in a mutually benefitting partnership between the two cultures.

Native American contributions to humanity's well-being have been immeasurable: agricultural products, architecture, clothing, crafts, literature, medicine, music, perfumes, place-names, and transportation. Through sign language, they established immediate communication between people speaking different tongues, a system other races are still searching for.

Contrary to general opinion, it was the Europeans who were humbled, and their arrogance diminished by being forced to council on native Americans' terms: it was native American etiquette and custom that prevailed and determined the agenda; it was their style of oratorical expression that was adopted. Many quotations in this volume amply demonstrate native American competence in negotiation, oratory and diplomacy equal to any known in political history. Consider, for example, that North American Indians are probably the only native race of any continent in the world to obtain concessions and payment from their adversaries for land forcibly occupied.

The problems that arose from land cessions were not caused by a lack of native American bargaining skills, but by the failure of Europeans, and later Euro-Americans, to uphold terms of the agreements. In time, native Americans were further disadvantaged as the white population increased and their own was reduced by lack of immunity to diseases contracted from whites—such as smallpox, murder, prejudice, and weakened physically from enforced removal to desolate areas where merely making the land habitable used up the tribes' energies.

Throughout this unfortunate period in native American history, the people depended on traditional principles underlying their philosophy for moral and spiritual fortitude. Additionally, some of the last remaining beautiful and natural areas of America are found on reservations. By example, native Americans have proven that theirs is a philosophy for present and future generations.

Creation:
The Great Circle Is The Universe

As we take the measure of the universe we minimize it, alienate it, struggle against it. But in learning of the world through the heart and feelings, as well as the mind, native Americans discerned a sense of unity within the macrocosm. The division of science and religion was unknown to them. There was only the Life Mystery to be learned; and as their experience and knowledge grew, so did their love for all creation, their humility before the infinite power of the Maker, their joy of kinship with every sentient being.

The perspective of the universe as the Great Circle becomes charged with a truth that is more than a physical fact, yet not merely a metaphysical concept. The chain of interdependence becomes sacred. The exchange of life-giving power transforms every commonplace act into a ritual of faith and solidarity. This perspective enhances understanding as we gaze at the great black bowl of the sky on a starry night and marvel at the all-encompassing roundness of it, or see the earth turning as the sun inches past the horizon.

Pleasant it looked, this newly created world. Along the entire length and breadth of the earth, our grandmother, extended the green reflection of her covering and the escaping odors were pleasant to inhale. (This Newly Created World, Winnebago)[1]

All things are the works of the Great Spirit. We should know that He is within all things; the trees, the grasses, the rivers, the mountains and all the four-legged animals, and the winged peoples; and even more important, we should understand that He is also above all these things and peoples. (Black Elk, Oglala Sioux)[2]

We are part fire, and part dream. We are the physical mirroring of Miaheyyun, the Total Universe, upon this earth, our Mother. We are here to experience. We are a movement of a hand within millions of seasons, a wink of touching within millions and millions of sun fires. And we speak with the Mirroring of the Sun.

The wind is the Spirit of these things. The force of the natural things of this world are brought together within the whirlwind. (Fire Dog, Cheyenne)[3]

The worship of the Great Mystery was silent, solitary, free from all self-seeking. It was silent because all speech is of necessity feeble and imperfect.... It was solitary, because they believed that He is nearer to us in solitude, and there were no priests authorized to come between a man and his Maker. None might exhort or confess or in any way meddle with the religious experience of another. Among us, all men were created sons of God and stood erect, as conscious of their divinity. Our faith might not be formulated in creeds, nor forced upon any who were unwilling to receive it; hence there was no preaching, proselytizing nor persecution; neither were there any scoffers or atheists.

There were no temples or shrines among us save those of nature.... He who enrobes Himself in filmy veils of cloud, there on the rim of the visible world where our Great-Grandfather Sun kindles his evening camp-fire, He who rides upon the rigorous wind of the north, or breathes forth His Spirit upon aromatic southern airs, whose war canoe is launched upon majestic rivers and inland seas—He needs no lesser cathedral. (Ohiyesa, Santee Sioux)[4]

You, whose day it is, make it beautiful. Get out your rainbow colors, so it will be beautiful. (Song to Bring Fair Weather, Nootka)[5]

The native vision, the gift of seeing truly, with wonder and delight into the natural world, is informed by a certain attitude of reverence and respect. It is a matter of extrasensory as well as sensory perception. In addition to the eye, it involves the intelligence, the instinct, and the imagination. It is the perception not only of objects and forms but also of essences and ideals. (N. Scott Momaday, Kiowa)[6]

Peace ... comes within the souls of men when they realize their relationship, their oneness, with the universe and all its powers, and when they realize that at the center of the Universe dwells

Wakan-Tanka, and that this center is really everywhere, it is within each of us. (Black Elk, Oglala Sioux)[7]

The greatest obstacle to the internal nature is the mind. If it relies on logic such as the white man's mind, the domain of the inner nature is inaccessible. The simple fact is a man does not challenge the wisdom of the Holy Mystery. (Turtleheart, Teton Sioux)[8]

We do not walk alone. Great Being walks beside us. Know this and be grateful. (Polingaysi Qoyawayma, Hopi)[9]

Wakonda! here, needy, he stands, and I am he. (*To Weep For Loss*, Omaha)[10]

Ho! Ye Sun, Moon, Stars, all ye that move in the heavens,
I bid you hear me!
Into your midst has come a new life.
    Consent ye, I implore!
Make its path smooth, that it may reach the brow of the
    first hill!
Ho! Ye Winds, Clouds, Rain, Mist, all ye that move in the air,
I bid you hear me!
Into your midst has come a new life.
    Consent ye, I implore!
Make its path smooth, that it may reach the brow of the
    second hill!
Ho! Ye Hills, Valleys, Rivers, Lakes, Trees, Grasses, all ye of the earth,
I bid you hear me!
Into your midst has come a new life.
    Consent ye, I implore!
Make its path smooth, that it may reach the brow of the
    third hill!
Ho! Ye Birds, great and small, that fly in the air,
Ho! Ye Animals, great and small, that dwell in the forest,
Ho! Ye Insects that creep among the grasses and burrow in the ground
I bid you hear me!
Into your midst has come a new life.
    Consent ye, I implore!
Make its path smooth, that it may reach the brow of the
    fourth hill!
Ho! All ye of the heavens, all ye of the air, all ye of the earth;
I bid you hear me!

Into your midst has come a new life.
    Consent ye all, I implore!
Make its path smooth—then shall it travel beyond the
    four hills!
(*Introduction of the Child to the Cosmos*, Pre-Columbian Ceremony,
Omaha)[11]

There are many secrets which the Great Mystery will disclose
only to the most worthy. Only those who seek him fasting and in
solitude will receive his signs. (Uncheedah, Santee Sioux)[12]

There was no such thing as emptiness in the world. Even in the
sky there were no vacant places. Everywhere there was life, visible
and invisible, and every object possessed something that would be
good for us to have also—even to the very stones. . . . The world
teemed with life and wisdom; there was no complete solitude for the
Lakota. (Luther Standing Bear, Lakota)[13]

He [the Great Spirit] only sketches out the path of life roughly
for all the creatures on earth, shows them where to go, where to
arrive at, but leaves them to find their own way to get there. He
wants them to act independently according to their nature, to the
urges in each of them. (John Fire/Lame Deer, Lakota)[14]

The chastisement of God is worse than any physical pain or
sickness. (Rosalio Moisés, Yaqui)[15]

At the edge of the cornfield a bird will sing with them in the
oneness of their happiness. So they will sing together in tune with
the universal power, in harmony with the one Creator of all things.
And the bird song, and the people's song, and the song of life will
become one. (*Song of the Long Hair Kachinas*, Hopi)[16]

The pipe was a tangible, visible link that joined man to Wakan-
Tanka, and every puff of smoke that ascended in prayer unfailingly
reached His presence. With it, faith was upheld, ceremony sanctified,
and the being consecrated. All the meanings of moral duty, ethics,
religious and spiritual conceptions were symbolized in the pipe. It
signified brotherhood, peace, and the perfection of Wakan-Tanka,
and to the Lakota the pipe stood for that which the Bible, Church,
State, and Flag, all combined, represented in the mind of the white
man. Without the pipe, no altar was complete and no ceremony
effective. It was used in council, all religious dance ceremonials, in

consecrating a life to the labor and service of band members, smoked by the scout to bind his word to truth, in salute and reverence to the rising sun, and by the man who mourned for the death of a loved one that it might dispatch grief and bring peace and solace. Smoking was the Indian Angelus, and whenever its smoke ascended, men, women, and children acknowledged the sacred presence of their Big Holy. (Luther Standing Bear, Lakota)[17]

Wakonda causes day to follow night without variation, and summer to follow winter; we can depend on these regular changes and can order our lives by them. In this way Wakonda teaches us that our words and our acts must be truthful, so that we may live in peace and happiness with one another. (oral tradition, Omaha)[18]

When we use water in the sweat lodge we should think of Wakan-Tanka who is always flowing, giving His power and life to everything; we should even be as water which is lower than all things, yet stronger even than the rocks. (Black Elk, Oglala Sioux)[19]

Follow Mother Earth in all things. See how she feeds her children, clothes and shelters them, comforts them with her good silence when their hearts have fallen down. Be like Mother Earth in all things. (village elder, Oglala Sioux)[20]

The Great Spirit first made the world, and next the flying animals, and found all things good and prosperous—He is immortal and everlasting. After finishing the flying animals, He came down on earth, and there stood. Then He made different kinds of trees and weeds of all sorts, and people of every kind. He made the spring and other seasons, and the weather suitable for planting. . . . When the Great Spirit had made the earth and its animals, He went into the great lakes, where He breathed as easily as anywhere else, and then made all the different kinds of fish. . . .

He is the cause of all things that exist, and it is very wicked to go against His will. . . . Some of us now keep the seventh day; but I wish to quit it, for the Great Spirit made it for others, but not for the Indians, who ought everyday to attend to their business. (Cornplanter, Seneca)[21]

We believed in a power that was higher than all people and all the created world, and we called this power the Man-Above. We believed in some power in the world that governed everything that grew, and we called this power Mother-Earth. We believed in the power of the Sun, of the Night-Sun or Moon, of the Morning Star, and of the Four Old Men who direct the winds and the rains and the seasons and give us the breath of life. We believed that everything created is holy and has some part in the power that is over all. (Carl Sweezy, Arapaho)[22]

What is gained from our inner nature is exact knowledge, which gives us a far-reaching outlook over the earth. The many powers of inner nature are hidden in everyone, and these are identified with Wakan-Tanka. (Blue Thunder, Teton Sioux)[23]

The hearts of little children are pure, and, therefore, the Great Spirit may show to them many things which older people miss. (Black Elk, Oglala Sioux)[24]

The first act of a man must be to set apart a place that can be made sacred and holy, that can be consecrated to Tirawa; a place where a man can be quiet and think—think about the mighty power and the place where the lesser powers dwell; a place where a man can put his sacred articles, those objects which enable him to approach the powers. (The Kurahus Tahirussawichi, Pawnee)[25]

A medicine man's visions were like other men's; but we gave them more heed, because we thought he had more power with the gods. We looked upon a medicine man as a prophet; his dreams and visions were messages to us from the spirits; and we thought of his mystery power as white men think of a prophet's power to work miracles. Our medicine men sought visions for us, and messages from the gods, just as white men's preachers study to tell them what God speaks to them in His book. (Edward Goodbird, Hidatsa)[26]

The Lakota thought of air much the same way as the white man does of water—something cleansing, something to bathe in. Our bodies bathed in air, and breathing was not only conducted through nose and lungs but with the entire body . . . bodies were nourished not only by food . . . wind, rain, and sun also nourished. (Luther Standing Bear, Lakota)[27]

I look at the Mother Earth as a relation of mine. I don't think people realize that our Mother Earth has a nervous system, just like a human body. I don't believe our fair Earth Mother can take anymore of the abuse that it has been forced to suffer by man. And when the nervous system of this planet is upset, it has to readjust itself, just

*like any other organism. The Earth Mother has to make its own
adjustments and retain its balance. And when it does this, there will
be catastrophies on its surface . . . and man is going to suffer.* (Dallas
Chief Eagle, Lakota)[28]

*They [the people] are children of Nature, and occasionally she
whips them with the lashes of experience, yet they are forgetful and
careless.* (Ohiyesa, Santee Sioux)[29]

*We may quarrel with men sometimes about things on earth,
but we never quarrel about the Great Spirit.* (Chief Joseph, Nez
Perce)[30]

*Brother, if you white men murdered the Son of the Great Spirit,
we Indians had nothing to do with it, and it is none of our affair. If he
had come among us, we would not have killed him; we would have
treated him well. You must make amends for that crime yourselves.*
(Red Jacket, Seneca)[31]

*All the powers that are in the heavens and all those that are
upon the earth are derived from the mighty power, Tirawa atius. He
is the father of all the lesser powers, those which can approach man.
He is the father of all the people and perpetuates the life of the tribe
through the gift of children.* (The Kurahus, Pawnee)[32]

*Deep down within us lingers a feeling that land, water, air, the
earth and what lives beneath its surface cannot be owned as
someone's private property. That belongs to everybody, and if man
wants to survive, he had better come around to this Indian point of
view, the sooner the better, because there isn't much time left to
think it over.* (John Fire/Lame Deer, Lakota)[33]

*Once in his life a man ought to concentrate his mind upon the
remembered earth. . . . He ought to give himself up to a particular
landscape in his experience, to look at it from as many angles as he
can, to wonder about it, to dwell upon it. He ought to imagine that
he touches it with his hands at every season and listens to the
sounds that are made upon it. He ought to imagine the creatures
there and all the faintest motions of the wind. He ought to recollect
the glare of noon and all the colors of the dawn and dusk.* (N. Scott
Momaday, Kiowa)[34]

*Mother Earth hears the call; she awakes; she arises; she feels the
breath of the new born Dawn. The leaves and the grass stir; all things*

move with the breath of the new day; everywhere life is renewed.
This is very mysterious; we are speaking of something very sacred,
although it happens every day. (The Kurahus, *Hako, Birth of Dawn*,
Pawnee)[35]

Flowers are for our souls to enjoy; not for our bodies to wear.
Leave them alone and they will live out their lives and reproduce
themselves as the Great Gardener intended. (oral tradition, Sioux)[36]

To us Indians, the spirit world seemed very near, and we did
nothing without taking thought of the gods. If we would begin a
journey, form a war party, hunt, trap eagles, or fish, or plant corn, we
first prayed to the spirits. A bad dream would send the bravest war
party hurrying home.

If our beliefs seem strange to white men, theirs seemed just as
strange to us. (Edward Goodbird, Hidatsa)[37]

The Cherokee lives as a natural part of his environment and
strives to complement it, not subdue or dominate it. It's an Indian
philosophy that is playing an increasing role in everyone's life now
that we realize that natural resources are limited and the imbalance
between man's technology and nature is perilously close to disaster.
(Huey P. Long, Cherokee)[38]

Man's heart away from nature, becomes hard; he [the Lakota]
knew that lack of respect for growing, living things soon led to lack
of respect for humans too. (Luther Standing Bear, Lakota)[39]

When you arise in the morning, give thanks for the morning
light, for your life and strength. Give thanks for your food and for
the joy of living. If you see no reason for giving thanks, the fault lies
in yourself. (Tecumseh, Shawnee)[40]

Nature, the Great Spirit—they are not perfect. The world
couldn't stand that perfection. The spirit has a good side and a bad
side. Sometimes the bad side gives me more knowledge than the
good side. (John Fire/Lame Deer, Lakota)[41]

Everything the Power of the World does is done in a circle. The
sky is round, and I have heard that the earth is round like a ball, and
so are all the stars. The wind in its greatest powers whirls. Birds make
their nests in circles, for theirs is the same religion as ours. The sun
comes forth and goes down again in a circle. The moon does the
same, and both are round. Even the seasons form a great circle in

their changing, and always come back where they were. The life of a man is a circle from childhood to childhood, and so it is in everything where power moves. (Black Elk, Oglala Sioux)[42]

White men think it strange that we Indians honored these sacred bundles; but I have heard that in Europe men once honored relics, the skull, or a bone, or a bit of hair of some saint, or a nail from Jesus' cross; that they did not pray to the relic, but thought that the spirit of the saint was near; or that he was more willing to hear their prayers when they knelt before the relic.

In much the same way, we Indians honored our sacred bundles. They contained sacred objects, or relics, that had belonged each to some god—his scalp, or skull, the pipe he smoked, or his robe. We did not pray to the object, but to the god or spirit to whom it had belonged, and we thought these sacred objects had wonderful power, just as white men once thought they could be cured of sickness by touching the bone of some saint. (Edward Goodbird, Hidatsa)[43]

Morality And Law:
Links In A Circle Without End

There was a certain inevitability about life, something un-
changeable to which the people accommodated themselves with
a sense of natural balance. Proper conduct was determined by
natural law made human which erased the distinction between
the "laws of nature" and the "rules of society." For both had
as their source the undeviating flow of events as humans and
nature reacted upon each other.

Nature was unpredictable, certainly, but the vagaries of
climate and environment, and the will to survive united the
people in a discovery of adaption to pulsating nature, and to
firmly plant those ways in their hearts and minds. Thus, human
law was a reflection, a response, an affirmation of natural law.

Practical knowledge to achieve right judgment and discern-
ment of acceptable behavior was an essential prerequisite to tribal
integration. Therefore, moral virtues as a quality of character
were strengthened through discipline of the mind and body.
Teaching by example developed the moral character of the individual, and by its extension, the moral virtues of the tribe. These
were reinforced by rewarding moral, physical and intellectual
excellence, and then emphasizing their relationship to nature in
religious rituals.

In a milieu in which personal integrity governed action and
reaction, native Americans did not require books of rules and
regulations to determine conduct.

*The people were put upon this world to learn of themselves and
of their brothers and sisters. We are these People. We are the Fallen
Star. Our laws of men change with our understandings of them.*

Only the laws of the Spirit remain always the same. (White Wolf, Crow)[44]

God said he was the Father and the Earth was the Mother of mankind; that nature was the law; that the animals and fish and plants obeyed nature and that man only was sinful. This is the old law. (Smowhala, Wanapum)[45]

Let me be a free man—free to travel, free to stop, free to work, free to trade where I choose, free to choose my own teachers, free to follow the religion of my fathers, free to talk and think and act for myself—and I will obey every law, or submit to the penalty. (Chief Joseph, Nez Perce)[46]

We believed in one God, the Great Spirit. We believed in our own kind of Ten Commandments. And we behaved as though we believed in them. (Reverend Vine Deloria, Sr., Yankton Sioux)[47]

In you, as in all men, are natural powers. You have a will. Learn to use it. Make it work for you. Sharpen your senses as you sharpen your knife. . . . We can give you nothing. You already possess everything necessary to become great. (Legendary Dwarf Chief, Crow)[48]

As we have reason, we have a right to use it in determining what is right or wrong; and should pursue that path which we believe to be right—believing that, "whatever is, is right." (Black Hawk, Sauk)[49]

I do not think that the measure of a civilization is how tall its buildings of concrete are, but rather on how well its people have learned to relate to their environment and fellow man. (Sun Bear, Chippewa)[50]

The song of the bird in the open tree is the one that brings true music to the ear, while that of the one in the cage is but a sad imitation. The one brings to its song something of the wide expanse of the sky, the voice of the wind, the sound of waters; the other's song can be only the song of captivity, of the bars that limit freedom, and the pain that is in the heart. (Old Keyam, Plains Cree)[51]

Standards of conduct were just as rigid as the laws of any other people, but force seldom was used to enforce good conduct. Each person was his own judge. Deceitfulness was a crime. We lived according to our own standards and principles, not for what others might think of us. Absolute honesty towards each other was the *basis of character. They knew nothing of what the white race calls "good breeding" and they had never heard of the "Golden Rule" but both principles were embodied in their intercourse with each other.* (Thomas Wildcat Alford, Shawnee)[52]

Our forefathers were under a strong persuasion (as we are) that those who act well in this life will be rewarded in the next according to the degrees of their virtues; and, on the other hand, that those who behave wickedly here will undergo such punishments hereafter as were proportionate to the crimes they were guilty of. This has been constantly and invariably received and acknowledged for a truth through every successive generation of our ancestors. It could not, then, have taken its rise from fable; for human fiction, however artfully and plausibly contrived, can never gain credit long among people where free inquiry is allowed, which was never denied by our ancestors. (anonymous chief, c. 1708, Conestoga)[53]

The first American mingled with his pride a singular humility. Spiritual arrogance was foreign to his nature and teaching. He never claimed that the power of articulate speech was proof of his superiority over the dumb creation; on the other hand, it is to him a perilous gift. He believes profoundly in silence—the sign of perfect equilibrium. Silence is the absolute poise and balance of body, mind, and spirit. The man who preserves his selfhood is ever calm and unshaken by the storms of existence... his, in the mind of the unlettered sage, is the ideal attitude and conduct of life.

If you ask him "What is silence?" he will answer "It is the Great Mystery! The holy silence is His voice!" If you ask "What are the fruits of silence?" he will say "They are self-control, true courage or endurance, patience, dignity, and reverence. Silence is the cornerstone of character." (Ohiyesa, Santee Sioux)[54]

Can things go well in a land where freedom of worship is a lie, a hollow boast? To each nation is given the light by which it knows God, and each finds its own way to express the longing to serve Him. . . . If a nation does not do what is right according to its own understanding, its power is worthless. (Thunderchild, Plains Cree)[55]

Some beliefs persist. The spirit may be enlightened, but the flesh is primeval.

Every nation has its superstitions, born in times when

ignorance was general, when people saw the world as through the eyes of childhood, when anything could have an air of unreality. Superstitions continue, and many believe in them even in these matter-of-fact days of more enlightment. (Old Keyam, Plains Cree)[56]

You [the white man] believe in the redeeming powers of suffering. . . . We believe that it is up to every one of us to help each other, even through the pain of our bodies. Pain to us is not "abstract," but very real. We do not lay this burden onto our god, nor do we want to miss being face to face with the spirit power. It is when we are fasting on the hilltop, or tearing our flesh at the Sun Dance, that we experience the sudden insight, come closest to the mind of the Great Spirit. Insight does not come cheaply, and we want no angel or saint to gain it for us and give it to us secondhand. (John Fire/Lame Deer, Lakota)[57]

The Indian's laws regarding his relationship with his fellow tribesmen were recorded in his heart. They were not written on tablets of stone or in law books. Each man carried the law in his heart. This is truly the only good law. (Sun Bear, Chippewa)[58]

There are four questions, which also serve as guidelines in self-discipline.

Ask yourself: (1) Am I happy in what I'm doing? (2) Is what I'm doing adding to the confusion? (3) What am I doing to bring about peace and contentment? (4) How will I be remembered when I am gone? (Twylah Nitsch, Seneca)[59]

Show respect for all men, but grovel to none. (Tecumseh, Shawnee)[60]

You [the women] have a hard life to live in this world, yet without you this life would not be what it is. Wakan-Tanka intends that you shall bear sorrow—comfort others in time of sorrow. By your hands the family moves. You have been given the knowledge of making clothing and of feeding the family. Wakan-Tanka is with you in your sorrows and joins you in your griefs. He has given you the great gift of kindness toward every living creature on earth. (White Buffalo Calf Woman, Teton Sioux)[61]

Face the rising sun with a cheerful spirit, as did our ancestors in the days of plenty. Then rain fell on all the land. But in these evil days it falls only on the fields of the faithful. (village elders, Hopi)[62]

Discipline from the young comes as from the earth and is accepted like hunger and weariness and the bite of winter cold. Coming so, it hatches no anger against the grown-up ones, no anger and hatred to sit in the heart like an arrow pointed to shoot both ways. (Bad Arm, Sioux)[63]

You will truly have good lives if you help each other. That is the way you could make each other happy . . . always feel willing to do for each other. This you are to do as long as the people's earth remains. (White Buffalo Dance, Fox)[64]

We were too uncivilized to set much value on personal belongings. We wanted to have things only in order to give them away. We had no money and therefore a man's worth couldn't be measured by it. (John Fire/Lame Deer, Lakota)[65]

You [Euro-Americans] have a very complicated legal system. It is not that way with my people. I have always thought that you had so many laws because you were a lawless people. . . . After all, Europe opened all prisons and penitentiaries and sent all their criminals to this country. Perhaps that is why you need so many laws. I hope we never have to reach such an advanced state of civilization. (Janet McCloud, Nisqualli)[66]

The apparent thing to the Lakota was that the written word was in itself ineffective and without power; and "woope," or what the white man called "law," designated not order but force and disorder. Force, no matter how concealed, begets resistance. (Luther Standing Bear, Lakota)[67]

The only things needing the protection of men are the things of men, not the things of the Spirit. (White Wolf, Crow)[68]

Good and evil cannot dwell together in the same heart, so a good man ought not to go into evil company. (Wingenim, Delaware)[69]

Even if the heavens were to fall on me, I want to do what is right. . . . I never do wrong without a cause. (Geronimo, Chiricahua Apache)[70]

He who is present at a wrongdoing, and lifts not a hand to prevent it, is as guilty as the wrongdoers. (Estamaza, Omaha)[71]

We are told by some thinkers that between the material and the spiritual parts of man there is a great division, that there is no shading of one into the other. I cannot believe that. One affects the other, and the place where a man lives can shape his character. (Old Keyam, Plains Cree)[72]

Our parents taught us that lying was the "great shame;" that it was the "battle-shield behind which the coward hid his shame." (Buffalo Child Long Lance, Sioux)[73]

I have already agreed to be there and that is the same as if I gave you my head and my heart. . . . I won't try to take back what I have said. I will do as I told you I would. (tribe member, Western Apache)[74]

Treachery darkens the chain of friendship; but truth makes it brighter than ever. (Conestoga Chief, 1706, Conestoga)[75]

In anger the will power is charged with evil and the man becomes dangerous to himself and to others. (oral tradition, Omaha)[76]

Stealing is a bad thing. One who is not in the habit of stealing easily continues to get property so that it will be his own. (Singing Around Rite, Fox)[77]

One never forgets to acknowledge a favor, no matter how small. (moral teaching, Omaha)[78]

Don't hug the earth; he who hugs the earth will soon be hugged by the earth. Be an early riser, the game do not snuggle their heads on feather pillows, they are out grazing at the break of dawn. Greet the newborn day. (Ochankugahe, Assiniboine)[79]

I seek strength, not to be greater than my brother, but to fight my greatest enemy—myself. . . . So when life fades, as the fading sunset, my spirit may come to you [Great Spirit] without shame. (anonymous, tribe unknown)[80]

Mother Corn has fed you, as she has fed all Hopi people, since long, long ago when she was no larger than my thumb. Mother Corn is a promise of food and life. I grind with gratitude for the richness of our harvest, not with cross feelings of working too hard. As I kneel at my grinding stone, I bow my head in prayer, thanking the great forces for provision. I have received much. I am willing to give much in return . . . there must always be a giving back for what one receives. (Sevenka Qoyawayma, Hopi)[81]

It is always good to do good, it is said. (Sam Blow Snake, Winnebago)[82]

Kindness is to use one's will to guard one's speech and conduct so as not to injure anyone. (oral tradition, Omaha)[83]

Indians never interrupt anyone when he is talking, even if he should talk all day—that is an ancient courtesy. (Buffalo Child Long Lance, Sioux)[84]

When a man gives of himself to those who are unfortunate, when his heart says, "I thank thee, Great Spirit," can one believe that nothing comes of it? (Thunderchild, Plains Cree)[85]

There are many ways our people worship the Great One. To the Sioux, all of the ways are good. We teach our children that the way is not as important as the belief. Only Wakan-Tanka himself knows which form is the most pleasing to him. (Blue Thunder, Teton Sioux)[86]

I believe the Great Spirit is always angry with men who shed innocent blood. (White Cloud, Iowa)[87]

First you are to think always of God, of Wakan-Tanka. Second, you are to use all your powers to care for your people, and especially for the poor. (Black Moon, Hunkpapa Sioux)[88]

I now know that the voice of man can reach to the sky;
I now know that the mighty one has heard as I prayed;
I now know that the gifts I asked have all granted been;
I now know that the word of old we truly have heard;
I now know that Tirawa harkens unto man's prayer;
I know that only good has come, my children, to you. (*Hako*, Fifteenth Ritual, Pawnee)[89]

In the Indian language we have no profane words. It has been said that before the advent of Christianity, the Indians did not know of the existence of God. It is true the missionaries have brought Christianity to my people, but may we not ask who brought blasphemy? (Ochankugahe, Assiniboine)[90]

Christians get drunk! Christians beat men! Christians tell lies! Me no Christian! (a young Chief, c. 1735, Cherokee)[91]

Live quietly. You must live gently. You must think kindly toward each other. Do not think of what is evil toward each other.

You must all be fond of each other. And do not think of bad language. . . . I desire you to do what is right, always what is right is what I desire of you. (Manito, Meskwaki)[92]

Trouble no man about his religion—respect him in his views, and demand that he respect yours. (Tecumseh, Shawnee)[93]

If there is one religion why do you white people disagree about it as you all read the same book? (Red Jacket, Seneca)[94]

I think the white people pray to the same Great Medicine we do in our old Cheyenne way. I do not go often to the church, but I go sometimes. I think the white church people are good, but I do not believe all of the stories they tell about what happened a long time ago. The way they tell us, all of the good people in the old times were white people. I am glad to have the white man churches among us, but I feel more satisfied when I make my prayers in the way I was taught to make them. My heart is much more contented when I sit alone with my medicine pipe and talk with the Great Medicine about whatever may be troubling me. (Wooden Leg, Cheyenne)[95]

When the Black Robes came to us they talked about the devil but we could not find him in the things we knew. We think that everything is good and bad and that no person or thing is all good or all bad. (Two Leggings, Crow)[96]

The Sun Dance started many years before Christopher Columbus drifted to these shores. We then knew that there was a God above us all. We called God "Wakan-Tanka," or the "Big Holy," or sometimes "Grandfather." You call God Father. I bring this before you because I want you to know that this dance was our religious belief. According to our legend, the red man was to have this dance every summer, to fulfill our religious duty. (Luther Standing Bear, Lakota)[97]

There is ahead of us a very great sorrow, at the time whenever it is daylight for the last time. Many people do not know it. They merely consider the joy of this day while we are alive. Yet all have been instructed but forget it; they think more of what is evil. (Singing Around Rite, Fox)[98]

A great many of our young people are floundering about. They have lost their bearings because they have lost the tenacious, underlying strength of their forefathers and have not attained any of their own. . . . In every human heart there is a deep spiritual hunger for an abiding, steadfast faith, a positive, satisfying belief in some future existence. Such a faith stabilizes character, and many of our young people have no such anchor for their souls. (Thomas Wildcat Alford, Shawnee)[99]

The white men have offered us two forms of their religion—the Roman Catholic and the Protestant—but we in our Indian lands had our own religion. Why is that not accepted too? It is the worship of one God, and it was the strength of our people for centuries.

I do not want to fight the white man's religion. I believe in freedom of worship, and though I am not a Christian, I have never forgotten God. What is it that has helped me and will help my grandchildren but belief in God?

He looks upon the wrong that is done on earth, and knows what would correct it. But we ourselves must find the way and do it. (Thunderchild, Plains Cree)[100]

We live, we die, and, like the grass and trees, renew ourselves from the soft clods of the grave. Stones crumble and decay, faiths grow old and they are forgotten, but new beliefs are born. The faith of the villages is dust now, but it will grow again like the trees. (Old One, Wanapum)[101]

Our entire Way of life will change. The coming of the white man will make this change. . . . But it will never die, because it is of the Spirit. It is a Truth, and Truth cannot die. (White Wolf, Crow)[102]

Wisdom:
The Circle Is The Great Medicine Wheel

In the English language, medicine is a therapeutic cure for illness affecting the body. To native Americans medicine was easily and naturally interchangeable with "holy" or "sacred." The inherent distinction is one of attitude toward the world and humankind's place within it.

Almost everything native Americans encountered in nature could be medicine that acted at once on the body, mind and spirit. All the ceremonies were medicine. Cultural and natural laws, when fully understood and lived, were medicine. Knowledge was medicine. Even proverbs, the elderly's advice, and striving to make life more satisfying were medicine.

The search for medicine often took heroic forms, like the vision quest in which a man or woman would fast and mortify the flesh, hoping some power would grant a vision, a transmission of wisdom. If successful, the seeker gathered natural specimens and special objects testifying to the power or wisdom received—this was the medicine bag. Many Euro-Americans find it difficult to comprehend the intermingling of belief, ritual, artistry, symbolism and spirituality which the medicine bag represented.

Medicine was the animating and formative principle underlying the native Americans' view of the cosmos. It was not a hypothesis for speculation, but rather a unifying force of perceived certainty.

The wisdom of native Americans reveals their understanding that harmony lies in reciprocity. Every act reflected its influence in kind on the doer. A deed or a thought thus traverses a circular path throughout creation until it is reabsorbed at its source.

As we learn we always change, and so does our perceiving. This changed perception then becomes a new Teacher inside each of us. Often our first Teacher is our own heart. (Hyemeyohsts Storm, Cheyenne)[103]

Each one must learn for himself the highest wisdom. It cannot be taught in words. (Smowhala, Wanapum)[104]

Just what Power is I cannot explain, for it is beyond my comprehension. Those who seek it go alone that they may be tested for worthiness. It is a gift to be bestowed not only for virtue but for prayer and courage. (Victorio, Mimbres Apache)[105]

When the mind is clear, discrimination is possible as are reasonable conclusions—it is the unclouded mind that can perceive what is conducive to the best in words and in deeds, to the attainment of wisdom. (oral tradition, Omaha)[106]

Knowledge is healing. If you help someone to a better knowledge so they can make a better life and living, then you are healing them. (Sun Bear, Chippewa)[107]

Develop your body, but do not neglect your mind. It is the mind that leads a man to power, not strength of body. (voice in a vision quest, Crow)[108]

Knowledge that is not used is abused. (Old Keyam, Plains Cree)[109]

"Truth is power," or, "Wowienke he iyotam wowa sake" as the Lakota spoke it. (adage, Lakota)[110]

The smarter a man is the more he needs God to protect him from thinking he knows everything. (George Webb, Pima)[111]

A medicine man has to be of the earth, somebody who reads nature as white men read a book. (John Fire/Lame Deer, Lakota)[112]

The eyes of living men speak words which the tongue cannot pronounce. (Plenty Coups, Crow)[113]

He gains success and avoids failure by learning how others succeeded or failed, and without trouble to himself. (voice in a vision quest, Crow)[114]

You ought to follow the example of shunktokecha (wolf). Even when he is surprised and runs for his life, he will pause to take one more look at you before he enters his final retreat. So you must take a second look at everything you see. (Uncheedah, Santee Sioux)[115]

Look twice at a two-faced man. (Chief Joseph, Nez Perce)[116]

Nobody wishes to be dependent upon others. . . . With gifts you make slaves just as with whips you make dogs! (anonymous, Eskimo)[117]

When the hearts of the givers are filled with hate, their gifts are small. (Plenty Coups, Crow)[118]

Free yourself from negative influence. Negative thoughts are the old habits that gnaw at the roots of the soul. (Moses Shongo, Seneca)[119]

One has to face fear or forever run from it. (Hawk, Crow)[120]

It is a truth, a melancholy truth, that the good things which men do are often buried in the ground, while their evil deeds are stripped naked and exposed to the world. (Black Thunder, Fox)[121]

Not only ignore by manner the people who annoy you, but learn to ignore in mind. For you they do not exist. You are free. (ethic, Cherokee)[122]

To peddle gossip is like playing checkers with an evil spirit. You win occasionally but you are more often trapped at your own game. (Don Talayesva, Hopi)[123]

Have patience. All things change in due time. Wishing cannot bring autumn glory nor cause winter to cease. (Ginaly-li, mystic, Cherokee)[124]

Finish what you begin. Those who leave things half done get boils on their heads. Do you want boils on your head? (Sevenka Qoyawayma, Hopi)[125]

Guard your tongue in youth and in age you may mature a thought that will be of service to your people! (Wabashaw, Mdewakanton Sioux)[126]

If a man is to do something more than human he must have more than human power. (a native American, tribe unknown)[127]

A brave man dies but once—cowards are always dying. (Moanahonga, Iowa)[128]

[When danger threatens] sit tight and perhaps in that way you may escape evil. (oral tradition, Navajo)[129]

Your mind must be like a tipi. Leave the entrance flap open so that the fresh air can enter and clear out the smoke of confusion. (Chiefeagle, Teton Sioux)[130]

You must have crooked ears; you have never done what I told you as you should. (White Buffalo, Fox)[131]

Do not open your mouth too widely but say something. (Sam Blow Snake, Winnebago)[132]

The longer a problem is allowed to exist, the harder it is to return to peace of mind. (Twylah Nitsch, Seneca)[133]

Poverty is a noose that strangles humility and breeds disrespect for God and man. (Wilbur Riegert, Sioux)[134]

Happiness is not only good in itself but is very healthful. (ethic, Hopi)[135]

Most of us do not look as handsome to others as we do to ourselves. (Fire Bear, Assiniboine)[136]

Try to do something brave. That man is most successful who is foremost. (Jumping Bull, Hunkpapa Sioux)[137]

There is a hole at the end of the thief's path. (proverb, Lakota)[138]

A man should rely on his own resources; the one who so trains himself is ready for any emergency. (ethic, Omaha)[139]

Everyone who is prosperous or successful must have dreamed of something. (Last Star, Maricopa)[140]

No one likes to be criticized, but criticism can be something like the desert wind that, in whipping the tender corn stalks, forces them to strike their roots down deeper for security. (Polingaysi Qoyawayma, Hopi)[141]

Strength is not the only thing we must have in the world, and, in a man or a nation, it is of little use without wisdom. (Chacopee and the Wooden Man, Yankton Sioux)[142]

A central wisdom, known to all Medicine doctors as a secret of the ages, asserts that self-understanding is a desire; that self-discipline is a key; self-control, a way; self-realization, the goal. The word that encompassed the secret is communication. There is a belief that everyone in every nation still acts as a guardian over this secret. (Twylah Nitsch, Seneca)[143]

We cannot reap happiness while wallowing in the mire of immaturity, because immaturity fosters emotional chaos, self-degradation and depravity. (Moses Shongo, Seneca)[144]

It is senseless to fight when you cannot hope to win. (Geronimo, Chiricahua Apache)[145]

The frog does not drink up the pond in which he lives. (proverb, Teton Sioux)[146]

Do not judge your neighbor until you walk two moons in his moccasins. (ancient proverb, Northern Cheyenne)[147]

If an innocent man doesn't get angry, he'll live a long while. A guilty man will get sick because of bad thoughts, a bad conscience. (traditional teaching, Hopi)[148]

Argument doesn't pay: you don't come home happy. (ethic, Hopi)[149]

The wildcat does not make enemies by rash action. He is observant, quiet, and tactful, and he always gains his ends. (oral teaching, Pawnee)[150]

Do not speak of evil for it creates curiosity in the minds of the young. (proverb, Lakota)[151]

Don't smoke until you have reached the age of thirty summers, as the nicotine will weaken your sinews, weaken your heart and make you short of breath, and you will be no match for the enemy when you come to grips with him. (tribal sage, Assiniboine)[152]

Bad thoughts are like jabbing at the thought-of-one with a knife. He can't see what you are doing to him, but you know, and killing someone in your thoughts will let evil spirits into you. (a mother's counsel, Hopi)[153]

Why had not my mother told me these things [that happened]? Why hadn't the shaman told me? Maybe it was another case of Indian philosophy: "Had you been there you would have known; you were not, so you do not need to know." (Niño Cochise, Chiricahua Apache)[154]

The selfish man is lonely, and his untended fire dies. (advice from a father, Pima)[155]

Great men are usually destroyed by those who are jealous of them. (Sitting Bull, Hunkpapa Sioux)[156]

One must learn from the bite of the fire to let it alone. (proverb, Sioux)[157]

To give up when all is against you, is a sign of being weak and cowardly. (Chiefeagle, Teton Sioux)[158]

Better that one only should suffer, than that all should perish. (The Little Spirit, Ojibwa)[159]

The old blood creeps with the snail, but the young blood leaps with the torrent. (Washakie, Shoshone)[160]

Be happy in order to live long. Worry makes you sick. (ethic, Hopi)[161]

Getting mad is a bad habit. (proverb, Hopi)[162]

The path of the lazy leads to disgrace. (proverb, Omaha)[163]

A man (or woman) with many children has many homes. (proverb, Lakota)[164]

When there is true hospitality, not very many words are needed. (Carl Sweezy, Arapaho)[165]

Touch not the poisonous firewater that makes wise men turn to fools and robs the spirit of its vision. (Tecumseh, Shawnee)[166]

If you sleep late your face will become wrinkled. (mother's traditional advice, Navajo)[167]

Stolen food never satisfies hunger. (proverb, Omaha)[168]

There are four ways in which you may go, if you are going somewhere. The first is to go immediately on first thought. That is not right. Think about it. This will make it the second way. Then think again about it a third time, but don't go yet. Then on the fourth consideration, go and it will be all right. Thus you will be safe. Sometimes wait a day in between considerations of your problems. (Diablo, White Mountain Apache)[169]

That people will continue longest in the enjoyment of peace who timely prepare to vindicate themselves and manifest a determination to protect themselves whenever they are wronged. (Tecumseh, Shawnee)[170]

It is not wise to differ in our tastes from other people; nor ought we to put off, through slothfulness, what is best done at once. Had Shawondasee conformed to the tastes of his countrymen, he would not have been an admirer of yellow hair; and if he had evinced a proper activity in his youth, his mind would not have run flower-gathering in his age. (Shawondasee, Ojibwa)[171]

[Revenge] might cause more trouble. Maybe you give him worse than he gave you, and then he makes it bigger. (ethic, Hopi)[172]

Everyone can be happy; even the most insignificant can have his song of thanks. (ancient holy man, Pawnee)[173]

Life And Death:
The Circle Is Timeless

It is a trait of human nature to continually question the purpose and destiny of existence. But the answer lies beyond human understanding, for it requires an omniscient knowledge of the cosmos, and of the ultimate power that governs it.

It is not life, but death, which goads us to seek the purpose for human existence. It is death that intensifies the joy of being alive; death that inspires a dynamic will to live.

The native Americans' attitude towards death provides an example of the language of the soul when humanity confronts the inevitable from its earthly citadel. Believing in life after death, native Americans can orient themselves to the universe and experience the quality of greatness, the virtue of courage, and the ecstasy of creation.

The native Americans' philosophy of death is the sum of their emotions, perceptions, and memories. It links them with a world-mind through its conception of human existence as unconstrained by time and place, secure in its constant oneness with the Creator.

Native Americans thus comprehend the harmony in the endless circle of creation and re-creation: their interred bodies return nourishment to the earth; the earth makes the plants grow; the plants feed the animals; the animals feed humanity.

Reflecting upon the remarkable pattern of causes and things caused, and upon the connection between the natural world and the essences beyond it, they stand in awe of it. They are humbled by it. It is a mystery.

Through the great corridor of the past, native Americans recall with respect the Old Ones who spoke wisely of life and death, the soul and the voice that filled Earth long before man was. They succumb to the Old Ones' inspiration.

What is life? It is the flash of a firefly in the night. It is the breath of a buffalo in the wintertime. It is the little shadow which runs across the grass and loses itself in the sunset. (Crowfoot, Blackfoot)[174]

It was the wind that gave them life. It is the wind that comes out of our mouths now that gives us life. When this ceases to blow we die. In the skin at the tips of our fingers we see the trail of the wind; it shows us where the wind blew when our ancestors were created. (It Was the Wind, Navajo)[175]

We do not know what may happen today, but let us act as though we were the Seven Stars (Big Dipper) in the sky that live forever. Go with me as far as you can, and I will go with you while there is breath in my body. (Plenty Coups, Crow)[176]

The centuries are for the young. For us old men, there is only one short hour. (Old One, Wanapum)[177]

Old age is not as honorable as death, but most people want it. (Two Leggings, Crow)[178]

So live your life that the fear of death can never enter your heart. (Tecumseh, Shawnee)[179]

You must live your life from beginning to end. No one else can do it for you. (old ones, Hopi)[180]

The Manitou thinks of you all alike. . . . Your lives are all of the same extent. No person's life is more than another's. You all have the same lives. No one knows when he will die. (White Buffalo Dance, Fox)[181]

In the beginning there was Life, and Life wanted to kill Poverty. Poverty said that if it were killed, Life would have nothing to do. So man spared Poverty. And it exists today. It keeps man occupied. (ancient legend, Navajo)[182]

All life was injustice. . . . Lightning found the good man and the bad; sickness carried no respect for virtue, and luck flitted around like the spring butterfly. It is good to learn this in the days of the mother's milk. (Bad Arm, Sioux)[183]

To the Thunder gods belongs the power to decree death and

man must conform his acts to the will of the gods even though his spirit chafes under restraint. (Hethu'shka Society tenet, Omaha)[184]

Men die but live again in the real world of Wakan-Tanka, where there is nothing but the spirits of all things; and this true life we may know here on earth if we purify our bodies and minds, thus coming closer to Wakan-Tanka who is all-purity. (Black Elk, Oglala Sioux)[185]

Let me see, if this be real, this life I am living! Ye who possess the skies, let me see if this be real, this life I am living. (death song, Pawnee)[186]

If you have always loved a person then when he dies you will have the right to feel sorry. (Sam Blow Snake, Winnebago)[187]

Love is something that you can leave behind you when you die. It's that powerful. (John Fire/Lame Deer, Lakota)[188]

When your time comes to die, be not like those whose hearts are filled with the fear of death, so when their time comes they weep and pray for a little more time to live their lives over again in a different way. Sing your death song, and die like a hero going home. (Tecumseh, Shawnee)[189]

No one has found a way to avoid death, to pass around it; those old men who have met it, who have reached the place where death stands waiting, have not pointed out a way to circumvent it. Death is difficult to face! (death song, Omaha)[190]

Man's life is transitory, and being so it is useless to harbor the fear of death, for death must come sooner or later to everybody; man and all living creatures come into existence, pass on, and are gone, while the mountains and rivers remain ever the same—these alone of all visible things abide unchanged. (Hethu'shka Society tenet, Omaha)[191]

Do not grieve. Misfortunes will happen to the wisest and best of men. Death will come and always comes out of season. It is the command of the Great Spirit, and all nations and people must obey. What is past and cannot be prevented should not be grieved for. . . . Misfortunes do not flourish particularly in our path. They grow everywhere. (Big Elk, funeral oration, Omaha)[192]

Don't be afraid to cry. It will free your mind of sorrowful thoughts. (Don Talayesva, Hopi)[193]

Nothing lives long. Only the earth and the mountains. (White Antelope, death song, Cheyenne)[194]

White men know much. And yet white men build great houses, as if they were to live forever. But white men cannot live forever. In a little time white men will be dust as well as I. (a young Chief, c. 1735, Cherokee)[195]

You must not cling to your sorrow nor hold an unkind feeling toward anyone. Have faith in yourselves and people will think more of you and Manido will help you. (White Feather, Ojibwa)[196]

It [death] cannot be helped. It is ever thus. Do not look where you have come from, but rather look forward to where you are to go.... (advice to a widow, Zuñi)[197]

With us it is a custom to visit the graves of our friends, and keep them in repair for many years. The mother will go alone to weep over the grave of her child! The brave, with pleasure, visits the grave of his father, after he has been successful in war, and re-paints the post that shows where he lies! (Black Hawk, Sauk)[198]

Wars are fought to see who owns the land, but in the end it possesses man. Who dares say he owns it—is he not buried beneath it? (Niño Cochise, Chiricahua Apache)[199]

At night when the streets of your cities and villages are silent and you think them deserted, they will throng with the returning hosts that once filled them and still love this beautiful land. The White Man will never be alone.

Let him be just and deal kindly with my people, for the dead are not powerless. Dead did I say? There is no death, only a change of worlds. (Seattle, Duwamish)[200]

The Family:
Circles Within Circles

In general, the family unit was the center of the network of relationships that included an entire tribe. Families formed economic as well as social communities, fulfilling the functions that public and private institutions perform in Euro-American society. Because of mutual dependence, all provisions needed for the people's welfare were held in common ownership. Collective ownership solidified the community since each member shared, in feast and famine, an intimate alliance with all other members. Such broad kinship provided an unending supply of affection and role models, especially for children. This was an important element in their unstructured method of education.

The native Americans' schoolroom was the world. The teachers were their family, friends and tribe elders. Lessons were learned not by rote, but by doing, even what we call "mistakes" were to them valuable additions to knowledge.

By the age of puberty, both males and females were well versed in their duties and obligations to ensure the survival of the family and tribe. The men were primarily occupied with obtaining game. Hunting forays sometimes required long journeys that kept them away for many days or weeks. For this reason, the women planted and harvested crops and performed other chores which their sedentary positions allowed.

Each individual knew the world's pleasure and attractions as well as hazards, and each was willing to temper self-gratification with a mix of mysticism and practicality.

I have always been a rich man. I have my family and we all have our good health. We have land to farm, houses to live in, food on our tables, and enough clothes. Most of all, we have the love in our hearts for each other and our friends. (Tsali, Cherokee)[201]

Be true to your blood and kin, even though death be the result. (tribal code, Assiniboine)[202]

There is a special magic and holiness about the girl and woman. They are the bringers of life to the people, and the teachers of the little children. (Sweet Medicine, Cheyenne)[203]

It is well to be good to women in the strength of our manhood because we must sit under their hands at both ends of our lives. (He Dog, Oglala Sioux)[204]

I've thought about men and women, and I always thought a man was bigger and stronger. . . .

I was that way for a long time, until I got gray hair; then I found out that a man is way behind and a woman is way ahead, because a woman can do all kinds of hard work too. I found out they're in many sufferings, and I found out that they can stand them. . . . She suffers a great deal through her generations.

When I found this out I thought, "A woman is stronger than a man." (Left Handed, Navajo)[205]

Because the woman bears the children, her side is to be favored. So, as the Hopi say, "The man is the slave." The clan is on the woman's side. (oral tradition, Hopi)[206]

When out together the man ought always to go first; it is his duty to see that the path is safe for the woman. (social etiquette, Omaha)[207]

Love songs are dangerous. If a man gets to singing them we send for a medicine man to treat him and make him stop. (anonymous tribesman, Papago)[208]

Look over the maidens among your people and make up your mind to one. I would advise that you do not pick out one who is too much for looks and has a good figure. Remember, if such a one gains favor in your eyes, she will also attract other men, and even though she sits beside you as your woman, men will continue to admire her just the same.

The relatives of your choice should be looked over to see if her men relations are good providers, skilled hunters, and men who are well-known. If her mother is neat and industrious, the daughter will be like her.

You must turn these things over in your mind many times when some good-to-look-at young woman tries to charm you. You may think you have made a good choice and want to hurry the marriage, but remember to take your time because the one you pick may cause you to live a miserable life.... Many things will make your heart heavy.

The good need not be told. You are grown up. Look around and see others. Be like the ones who live in happiness and contentment. (traditional grandfather's advice, Assiniboine)[209]

Women cannot be watched. If you try to watch them and are jealous about them... when your jealousy has developed to the highest pitch, your wife will leave you.... Because of this incessant annoyance she will run away.... You have likewise made the woman suffer; you have made her unhappy. The whole world will hear about it. (Sam Blow Snake, Winnebago)[210]

You must not bother with any woman or girl who is married to another man. You should not try to cut him out! It is dangerous to do that. (Harry Lincoln, Meskwaki)[211]

A person who does evil things... has disgraced his family. (moral tradition, Tlingit)[212]

Indians often used the mother's name and not the father's. When this was discovered by a white agent, he forced the Indian to supply the father's name instead. During one such incident, an old chief in South Dakota protested to the agent, "We have seen that the white man makes his women like toys, like pets. Now we see they are possessions, without names of their own." (anecdote, Sioux)[213]

A family may have disputes, but because of sickness they should forgive one another. (Namet, Maricopa)[214]

A Pima can laugh at himself. It is one way of seeing the other fellow's point of view. (George Webb, Pima)[215]

If you need something of your cousin, he is sure to give it to you.... If you have anything and your cousin needs it, he comes and asks for it and you give it to him. You can't refuse. (ancient ethic, Jicarilla Apache)[216]

You can't get rich if you look after your relatives right. (tribe leader, Navajo)[217]

Within every man there is the Reflection of a Woman, and within every woman there is the Reflection of a Man. Within every man and woman there is also the Reflection of an Old Man, and Old Woman, a Little Boy, and a Little Girl. (Hyemeyohsts Storm, Cheyenne)[218]

No indiscretion can banish a woman from her parental lodge—no difference how many children she may bring home, she is always welcome—the kettle is over the fire to feed them. (Black Hawk, Sauk)[219]

It is not only now that woman causes trouble. That has been since first man was. (Father of Thunderchild, Plains Cree)[220]

If you do bad things your children will follow you and do the same. If you want to raise good children, be decent yourself. (Chris, Mescalero Apache)[221]

A child believes that only the action of someone who is unfriendly can cause pain. (Chased-by-Bears, Santee Sioux)[222]

Good acts done for the love of children become stories good for the ears of people from other bands; they become as coveted things, and are placed side by side with the stories of war achievements. (social tradition, Assiniboine)[223]

Training began with children who were taught to sit still and enjoy it. They were taught to use their organs of smell, to look when there was apparently nothing to see, and to listen intently when all seemingly was quiet. A child that cannot sit still is a half-developed child. (Luther Standing Bear, Lakota)[224]

What do you do to a child that cries all the time? We don't do anything to the child. We hire a shaman to find out what is the matter with it and cure it, for, if something was not wrong, it wouldn't cry that way. (anonymous, Western Apache)[225]

Punishing children may make them sick and die ... injury of the body in any way is against the rules; you might hurt a person. (ethic, Hopi)[226]

Young children were scolded or lightly punished—the pulling of an ear or switching on the legs—when they disobeyed, falsified, or caused damage in the home. But children above six or seven years of age were expected to know the rules of proper behavior. (Peter Sconchin, Modoc)[227]

The pride of ownership, the desire to improve and to develop what he has, should be encouraged in a boy while he is young. (Old Keyam, Plains Cree)[228]

My brothers always stopped me when I was doing wrong. They had to. A boy can't learn good if he isn't. (Charles James Nowell, Kwakiutl)[229]

It is better to use ridicule early—to keep the young on the good road. (Bad Arm, Sioux)[230]

When a mother saw that her daughter was willing to listen to a foolish girl, she would say to her, "Whatever that foolish girl leads you to will be seen on you as long as you live." (a mother's counsel, Tlingit)[231]

Not until they [her cubs] almost freeze to death will she bring them inside. That's how the bear makes himself tough. The bear can stand anything; he's brave and unafraid. That's the way we must be, too. That's why we should do the same.
That's what all the racing and bathing is for. (Left Handed, Navajo)[232]

When company comes to our lodge, play outside and don't listen to grownups when they are talking, as you may thoughtlessly repeat some bit of gossip and cause trouble between families. (social tradition, Assiniboine)[233]

Teaching a young girl to make blue cornmeal dumplings: "Now, as you knead this dough in your warm hands, bear good thoughts in your heart, that there be no stain of evil in the food. Ask that it may have in it the greatness and power of Mother Earth, then those who eat it will be nourished in spirit as well as in body." (Polingaysi Qoyawayma, Hopi)[234]

You never know what girl will make you the best wife until after marriage, when she starts to cook. (anonymous, Western Apache)[235]

Nowadays they tell girls to look around for boys that have horses, homes, everything they want. They say, "That's the right kind of a man to marry—one that can support you." (Harry Lincoln, Meskwaki)[236]

Know enough about a boy before you admire him too much. The good-looking boy may be just good in the face. (proverb, Apache)[237]

See how the boy is with his sister and the other ones of his home lodge and you can know how the man will be with your daughter. (proverb, Plains Sioux)[238]

If you are industrious like the spider; if you are wise like the turtle; if you are cheerful like the lark, then you will be chosen by a brave man, and you will have plenty and never be ashamed. (Buffalo Ceremony Conductor, Oglala Sioux)[239]

On you [the men] it depends to be a strong help to the women in the raising of children. Share the Women's sorrow. Wakan-Tanka smiles on the man who has a kind feeling for a woman. (White Buffalo Calf Woman, Teton Sioux)[240]

It is the office of man to kindle the fire, but the part of woman to keep it burning. (ethic, Pima)[241]

If a man is out on a hunt or raid and sees that a lizard or horned toad is trying to get in bed with him, he knows that his wife is unfaithful to him. (Chris, Mescalero Apache)[242]

When you get married do not make an idol of the woman you marry; do not worship her. If you worship a woman she will insist upon greater and greater worship as time goes on. (Sam Blow Snake, Winnebago)[243]

I never did get a woman that thought the way I did. It's like a guessing game. If you don't know anything about it, you guess wrong and lose. (Old Mexican, Navajo)[244]

Marriage among my people was like traveling in a canoe. The man sat in front and paddled the canoe. The woman sat in the stern but she steered. (a native American, tribe unknown)[245]

It was understood that a man would give his bride time to adjust to the new routine: "Aproach the maiden as one would approach any shy creature of the earth, gently, slowly, one step at a time, as one approaches a young antelope trembling in a cactus patch, for the shy heart is the same." (social ethic, Sioux)[246]

There was a rigid rule for the old one in the young home: respect your place. Advice unasked makes the fire smoke. (Contrary's widow, Sioux)[247]

No one continues to be taken care of forever. The time soon comes when we lose sight of the one who takes care of us. (tribe mother, Fox)[248]

We respected our old people above all others in the tribe. To live to be so old they must have been brave and strong and good fighters, and we aspired to be like them. We never allowed our old people to want for anything. . . . We looked upon our old people as demigods of a kind, and we loved them deeply; they were all our fathers. (Buffalo Child Long Lance, Sioux)[249]

Look at your neighbor and make him sparkle. Your eyes are the mirror of your soul. When you sparkle your eyes, whether you think you are beautiful or not, you are. (Twylah Nitsch, Seneca)[250]

Men push people away from themselves in their loneliness and are afraid, causing them even more loneliness. Understanding is what these men crave. Give them understanding and they will respond to your companionship. (Hawk, Crow)[251]

Do not kill or injure your neighbor, for it is not him that you injure, you injure yourself. But do good to him, therefore add to his days of happiness as you add to your own.

Do not wrong or hate your neighbor, for it is not him that you wrong, you wrong yourself. But love him, for Moneto loves him also as He loves you! (Thomas Wildcat Alford, Shawnee)[252]

Sometime you may be desired as a son-in-law. But if you bother with many girls, while going with one, they will think you are a nobody. (Harry Lincoln, Meskwaki)[253]

The white man's mother-in-law problem, real or otherwise, is no problem to the Indian. Traditional custom prohibits communication between them. (Ochankugahe, Assiniboine)[254]

The Indians had their little "triangle affairs," but they were much better taken care of than by the white man's method. The chiefs always gave presents, from the one who was at fault to the other, who was to forgive and forget. If they could not do this, then they were not to go back together again. There was no great scandal written up in the papers about either party. It was up to them to do just as they thought best, and they lived happy, whether they were together or living apart. (Luther Standing Bear, Lakota)[255]

As a man is climbing up he does something that marks a place in his life where the powers have given him the opportunity to express in acts his peculiar endowments, so this place, this act, forms a stage in his career, and he takes a new name to indicate that he is on a level different from that which he occupied previously. Some men can rise only a little way, others live on a dead level. Men having power to advance, climb step by step. (The Kurahus Tahirussawichi, Pawnee)[256]

The Tribe:
The Circle Binds The People Together

The circle as a geometric form is unique among all those which the human mind can describe. It is the most natural, the one shape found everywhere in creation; a symphony of symmetry to highlight the curious architecture of the human figure, plants, and animals.

In the past, native Americans generally spent some part of their lives in circular dwellings. When migrant bands regrouped, the entire tribe came together to re-form the hoop of the nation; each band, each circle of homes and relations, had its place within the Great Circle comprising all the people. Sometimes this was an open circle, like the young crescent moon, with its points facing the dawn. Such gatherings re-established the bonds that united the people as a nation. Though outwardly different, all tribes had a circular pattern of renewing themselves mentally, physically, and spiritually.

Between periodic nationwide rites, there were countless occasions for the people to reaffirm their unity. In sweat lodges, participants sat close together around steaming rocks placed in a circle that enclosed a representation of the universe. The pipe passed from hand to hand with prayer offerings for tribe and kin. When chiefs met in council, they gathered in a round lodge with open walls. Outside, men and women formed a ring symbolizing the togetherness of the people, in a voluntary and spontaneous association to attain both the individual and the common good.

This talk is intended for all the different tribes of our red brothers, and is to last to the end of time. . . . I have made a fire out of the dry elm—this fire is for all the different tribes to see by. . . .

This fire is not to be extinguished so long as time lasts. I shall stick up a stick close by this fire, in order that it may frequently be stirred, and raise a light for the rising generation to see by; if any one should turn in the dark, you must catch him by the hand, and lead him to the light, so that he can see that he was wrong.

I have made you a fire-light, I have stripped some white hickory bark and set it up against the tree, in order that when you wish to remove this fire, you can take it and put it on the bark; when you kindle this fire it will be seen rising up toward the heavens.... I have prepared white benches for you, and leaned the white pipe against them, and when you eat you shall have but one dish and one spoon.... Where there is blood spilt I will wipe it up clean—where-ever bones have been scattered, I have taken them and buried them, and covered them with white hickory bark and a white cloth—there must be no more blood spilt. (Wampum Belt message, Shawnee)[257]

Father, the Sun, I am praying for my people.
May they be happy in the summer and live through the cold
    of winter.
Many are sick and hungry,
Pity them and let them live.
May we go through this ceremony right,
The way you taught our people to do in the days of long ago.
If we make mistakes, pity us.
Mother Earth, pity us, help us; may the grass and berries
    grow.
Morning Star, shine into our lodge and give us long life.
Father, the Sun, bless our children, relatives and visitors.
May our trails lie straight through a happy life; may we
    live to be old.
We are all your children and ask these things with good
    hearts. (White Calf, Sun Dance prayer, Blackfoot)[258]

We most truly honour what is past, when we seek in our changed conditions to attain the same proficiency that our fathers showed in their day and in their lives. (Edward Ahenakew, Plains Cree)[259]

To make sure that all the leaders and officers would be present at a gathering, the camp crier visited the lodge of each one and took away an object that was highly valued by the owner. When the owners attended, they received their objects back. The articles of those not present when the crier first announced the names of the owners were destroyed in full view of the audience as a warning. (First Boy, Assiniboine)[260]

Chiefs, headmen, and braves were known only by the places they occupied opposite the door of the hall, and sometimes the greatest among them had the least to say and remained the most inconspicuous. (Luther Standing Bear, Lakota)[261]

To be a great people is not just to be fine hunters and famous warriors. The Great Spirit thinks it is far more important for us to be good and kind to one another, so that we don't look down on other people, but help them with love and understanding. (Sweet Medicine, Cheyenne)[262]

A people without a history is like wind on the buffalo grass. (proverb, Teton Sioux)[263]

Every struggle, whether won or lost, strengthens us for the next to come. It is not good for people to have an easy life. They become weak and inefficient when they cease to struggle. Some need a series of defeats before developing the strength and courage to win a victory. (Victorio, Mimbres Apache)[264]

Let me do the right things for my people. Not for the sake of merit, but because of the sacrifice of my people in this land which belongs to them. (vision quest prayer, Teton Sioux)[265]

This I am telling you was told me by my grandmother, and before she told it to me she heard it from her grandmother, and before that her grandmother heard it from another old person. You white people have written books, but everything we know about our people is written in our heads. (an elderly Apache, Western Apache)[266]

Stories are a circle of believable dreams and oratorical gestures showing the meaning between the present and the past in the life of the people. The stories change as the people change, because people, not facts, are the center of the anishinabe world. (Ted D. Mahto, Chippewa)[267]

Don't be talkative, sooner or later it will have an adverse effect on you and the listeners. People will ask each other whether there

*was anything else you could do besides gabbing. . . . Deeds speak
louder than words.* (tribal sage, Assiniboine)[268]

*I wish I could live again through some of the past days when it
was the first thought of every prospering Indian to send out the
call: Hoh-oh-oh-oh, friends: Come. Come. Come. I have plenty of
buffalo meat. I have coffee. I have sugar. I have tobacco. Come,
friends, feast and smoke with me.* (Wooden Leg, Cheyenne)[269]

*When food was brought into the village, the sharing must be
equal for young, old, sick, disabled, and for all those who did not or
could not hunt as well as those who hunted. There must be no
hungry individuals; so long as one had food, all would have food.
There was never the hungry on one hand and the overfed on the
other. All shared food as long as there was any to share. If a hunter
disobeyed the custom of sharing and was caught making away
with game, he was severely punished by the Fox Lodge.* (Luther
Standing Bear, Lakota)[270]

*We aren't divided up into separate, neat little families—Pa, Ma,
kids, and to hell with everybody else. The whole damn tribe is one
big family; that's our kind of reality.* (John Fire/Lame Deer,
Lakota)[271]

*If an Apache had allowed his aged parents to suffer for food or
shelter, if he had neglected or abused the sick, if he had profaned our
religion, or had been unfaithful, he might be banished from the tribe.*
(Geronimo, Chiricahua Apache)[272]

*The honor of the people lies in the moccasin tracks of the
women. Walk the good road. . . . Be dutiful, respectful, gentle and
modest, my daughter. And proud walking. . . . Be strong, with the
warm, strong heart of the earth. No people goes down until their
women are weak and dishonored, or dead upon the ground. Be
strong and sing the strength of the Great Powers within you, all
around you.* (village wise man, Sioux)[273]

*It is in peace only that our women and children can enjoy
happiness and increase in numbers.* (John Ross, Cherokee)[274]

*When this pipe touches your lip, may it operate as a blessing
upon all my tribe. May the smoke rise like a cloud, and carry away
with it all the animosities which have arisen between us.* (Black
Thunder, Fox)[275]

I have been to the end of the earth.
I have been to the end of the waters.
I have been to the end of the sky.
I have been to the end of the mountains.
I have found none that were not my friends. (Song of the Young War
God. Navajo)[276]

There was a length and a breadth and a height to their lives. . . .
No wonder Columbus admired Indians, as did other explorers, and
George Catlin, who said such wonderful things. (Reverend Vine
Deloria, Sr., Yankton Sioux)[277]

If you have One Hundred People who Live Together, and if
Each One Cares for the Rest, there is One Mind. (Shining Arrows,
Crow)[278]

The Human Race:
The Circle Unites The People As One Nation

Contradictory religious and philosophical views have been one of the major causes of conflict between nations. It was such a difference in religious interpretation that embroiled Europe in almost four hundred years of constant warfare from the thirteenth to the seventeenth century.

The same religious intolerance which divided Europe resulted in the subjugation of native Americans in the Western Hemisphere.

Hostilities among the English, French, and Spanish settlements in the New World corresponded to the coalitions and wars in Europe. Inevitably, native Americans suffered greatly from the foreign-bred wars, and from the pursuit for their allegiance by contending Europeans. As a result of these rivalries, Indian nations were divided into bitterly opposing factions. Some small tribes disappeared completely as their people either were annihilated or else intermarried with the white and black races.

A love-hate relationship characterizes the dispute between Europeans and native Americans. It is a moral argument related to the rights of both: the oppressors, and the victims of historical circumstance. Native Americans were not well understood by Europeans, whose prejudices obscured the validity of traditions which seemed different from their own. Thus, they crystalized a misconceived image of native American societies, of the limited authority vested in tribal chiefs, and most devastating of all, of concepts regarding individual and group use of land.

The Old Ones taught that people, regardless of race, and by virtue of their common humanity, constitute one of the greater circles within the circular cosmos. Native Americans had not lost sight of this truth, but paid dearly for their optimism—genocide and degradation were their rewards as Europeans plundered the continent.

Through it all, native Americans sadly endured the rape of the beloved land of their ancestors. The Euro-Americans' self-inflicted wounds are finally causing them sufficient pain to awaken to the extent of their loss: the long-forgotten primeval conscience which informed them of their oneness with nature. On the edge of their thoughts the ignored message rankles for recognition of the waste that marks their path through the centuries. The ugliness should no longer be tolerated or avoided.

Realizing the folly of their actions, some Euro-Americans now look with irony and despair to their victims, the guardians of the spiritual covenant with nature, and earnestly wish to repair the misshaped hoop.

We Indians hold the pipe of peace . . . and we have stood by while the white man supposedly improved the world. Now we Indians must show how to live with our brothers, not use them, kill them, or maim them. . . .

We must try to use the pipe for mankind, which is on the road to self-destruction. We must try to get back on the red road of the pipe, the road of life. We must try to save the white man from himself. This can be done only if all of us, Indians and non-Indians alike, can again see ourselves as part of this earth, not as an enemy from the outside who tries to impose its will on it. . . . Maybe through this sacred pipe we can teach each other again to see through that cloud of pollution which politicians, industrialists and technical experts hold up to us as "reality." Through this pipe, maybe, we can make peace with our greatest enemy who dwells deep within ourselves. With this pipe we could all form again the circle without end. (John Fire/Lame Deer, Lakota)[279]

No man should seek to destroy the special genius that race ancestry gives him. The God of nations did not give races distinctive racial endowments and characteristics for naught. And now with a coming race-consciousness the American Indian seeks to go even further and say, "I am not a red man only, I am an American in the truest sense, and a brother man to all human kind." (Arthur C. Parker, Seneca)[280]

It is our Desire that we and you should be as of one Heart, one Mind, and one Body, thus becoming one People, entertaining a mutual Love and Regard for each other, to be preserved firm and entire, not only between you and us, but between your Children, and our Children, to all succeeding Generations.

We who are now here, are old Men, who have the Direction of Affairs in our own Nations; and as we are old, it may be thought that the Memory of these things may be lost with us, who have not, like you, the Art of preserving it by committing all Transactions to Writing: We nevertheless have Methods of transmitting from Father to Son, an Account of all these Things, whereby you will find the Remembrance of them is faithfully preserved, and our succeeding Generations are made acquainted with what has passed, that it may not be forgot as long as the Earth remains. (Kanickhungo, Iroquois)[281]

You will forgive me if I tell you that my people were Americans for thousands of years before your people were. The question is not how you can Americanize us, but how we can Americanize you. We have been working at that for a long time. Sometimes we are discouraged at the results. But we will keep trying. And the first thing we want to teach you is that, in the American way of life, each man has respect for his brother's vision. Because each of us respected his brother's dream, we enjoyed freedom here in America while your people were busy killing and enslaving each other across the water. The relatives you left behind are still trying to kill each other because they have not learned there that freedom is built on my respect for my brother's vision and his respect for mine. We have a hard trail ahead of us in trying to Americanize you and your white brothers. But we are not afraid of hard trails. (a native American, tribe unknown)[282]

I don't want a white man over me. I don't want an agent. I want to have the white man with me, but not to be my chief. (Sitting Bull, Hunkpapa Sioux)[283]

The troubles spring from seed. The seed was sown long ago by the white man not attending truthfully to his treaties after a majority of our people had voted for them. When the white man speaks, the government and the army see that we obey. When the red man speaks, it goes in at one ear and out of the other. (Young Man Afraid Of His Horse, Oglala Sioux)[284]

What is the matter that you don't speak to me? It would be better if you would speak to me and look with a pleasant face. It would make better feeling. I would be glad if you did. I'd be better satisfied if you would talk to me once in a while. Why don't you look at me and smile at me? I am the same man; I have the same feet, legs, and hands, and the sun looks down on me a complete man. I want you to look and smile at me. (Geronimo, Chiricahua Apache)[285]

We, who are clay blended by the Master Potter, come from the kiln of Creation in many hues. How can people say one skin is colored, when each has its own coloration? What should it matter that one bowl is dark and the other pale, if each is of good design and serves its purpose well? (Polingaysi Qoyawayma, Hopi)[286]

Let my father listen to justice and let him grant what is just to his red children. The color of the skin makes no difference; what is good and just for one is good and just for the other. (White Shield, Arikara)[287]

I shall not speak with fear and trembling. I have never injured you, and innocence can feel no fear. . . . It is a fact which can easily be proved, that I have been assailed in almost every possible way that pride, fear, feeling, or interest, could touch me—that I have been pushed to the last to raise the tomahawk against you; but all in vain. I never could be made to feel that you were my enemy. If this is the conduct of an enemy, I shall never be your friend. (Black Thunder, Fox)[288]

Fair is the clear sky, the green grass, yet more fair is peace among men. (Wawan Ceremony, Omaha)[289]

See there! look! You have killed all that was dear to me—my brother, my brother's wife, and her child. See the blood—it flows before you. Look at that woman; her arm was never raised against an American; the child never wronged you—it was innocent; they have gone to the Great Spirit. I came to meet you with the pipe of peace in my mouth. I did you no wrong; you fired upon me, and see what you have done—see my own wife with her head bleeding; though not dead, she is wounded. Now listen—you are not a brave, you are a dog. If you were a brave, I would treat you as a brave, but as you are a dog, I will treat you as a dog! (Moanahonga, Iowa)[290]

Some time ago you [the English] put a war hatchet into my hands, saying, "Take this weapon and try it on the heads of my enemies, the Long-Knives [colonists], and let me afterwards know if it was sharp and good." Father, at the time when you gave me this weapon, I had neither cause nor inclination to go to war against a people who had done me no injury; yet in obedience to you, who say you are my father, and call me your child, I received the hatchet; well knowing, that if I did not obey, you would withhold from me the necessaries of life, without which I could not subsist, and which are not elsewhere to be procured, but at the house of my father. —You may perhaps think me a fool, for risking my life at your bidding, in a cause too, by which I have no prospect of gaining anything; for it is your cause and not mine. It is your concern to fight the Long-Knives; you have raised a quarrel amongst yourselves, and you ought yourselves to fight it out. You should not compel your children, the Indians, to expose themselves to danger, for your sake. —Father, many lives have already been lost on your account! —Nations have suffered, and been weakened! —Children have lost parents, brothers, and relatives! —Wives have lost husbands! —It is not known how many more may perish before your war will be at an end! —Father, I have said, that you may, perhaps, think me a fool, for thus thoughtlessly rushing on your enemy! —Do not believe this, father: think not that I want sense to convince me, that although you now pretend to keep up a perpetual enmity to the Long-Knives, you may before long conclude a peace with them. —Father, you say you love your children, the Indians. —This you have often told them, and indeed it is your interest to say to them, that you may have them at your service. But, father, who of us can believe that you can love a people of a different color from your own, better than those who have a white skin like yourselves? Father, pay attention to what I am going to say. While you, father, are setting me on your enemy, much in the same manner as a hunter sets his dog on the game; while I am in the act of rushing on that enemy of yours, with the bloody destructive weapon you gave me, I may, perchance, happen to look back to the place from whence you started me; and what shall I see? Perhaps I may see my father shaking hands with the Long-Knives; yes, with these very people he now calls his enemies. I may then see him laugh at my folly for having obeyed his orders; and yet I am now risking my life at his command!

Father, keep what I have said in remembrance. (Hopocan, Delaware)[291]

I could once animate my warriors to battle—but I cannot animate the dead. My warriors can no longer hear my voice. Their bones are at Talladega, Tallushatches, Emuckfaw and Tohopeka. I have not surrendered myself without thought. While there was a single chance of success, I never left my post, nor supplicated peace. But my people are gone, and I now ask it for my nation, not for myself. I look back with deep sorrow, and wish to avert still greater calamities. If I had been left to contend with the Georgia [State] army, I would have raised my corn on one bank of the river, and fought them on the other. But your people have destroyed my nation. (William Weatherford, Creek)[292]

They [the Sioux] never tried to make a science of war . . . as it is today. Today we see all of the ingenuity of man, all of the inventiveness and craftiness of man turned to ends of destruction.

The Sioux's only efforts at warfare were to keep his boundaries intact. (Warcaziwin, Sioux)[293]

I was not hostile to the white men.

We had buffalo for food, and their hides for clothing and for our tipis. We preferred hunting to a life of idleness on the reservation, where we were driven against our will. At times we did not get enough to eat, and we were not allowed to leave the reservation to hunt.

We preferred our own way of living. We were no expense to the government. All we wanted was peace and to be left alone. Soldiers were sent out in the winter, who destroyed our villages.

Then Long Hair [George Custer] came in the same way. They say we massacred him, but he would have done the same thing to us had we not defended ourselves and fought to the last. Our first impulse was to escape with our women and children, but we were so hemmed in we had to fight.

After that I went up on the Tongue River with a few of my people and lived in peace. But the government would not let me alone. Finally I came back to the Red Cloud Agency. Yet I was not allowed to remain quiet.

I was tired of fighting. I went to the Spotted Tail Agency and asked that chief and his agent to let me live there in peace. I came here with the agent [Jesse M. Lee] to talk with the Big White Chief but was not given a chance. They tried to confine me. I tried to escape, and a soldier ran his bayonet into me. I have spoken. (Crazy Horse, Oglala Sioux)[294]

In 1794 a Western chief was presented with a presidential peace medal. The obverse side had an engraving of George Washington armed with a sword. The reverse depicted an Indian burying a hatchet. The chief, noting the poses, asked: Why does not the president bury his sword, too? (anonymous native American, tribe unknown)[295]

Experience is the wisest teacher, and history does not furnish an example of a forced civilization being permanent and real. (Pleasant Porter, Creek)[296]

Why should you take by force that from us which you can have by love? (Wahunsonacock (Powhatan), Powhatan)[297]

Well, as the great chief [President Madison] is to decide the matter, I hope the Great Spirit will put sense enough into his head to induce him to direct you to give up this land. It is true, he is so far off he will not be injured by the war; he may sit still in his town and drink his wine, while you and I will have to fight it out. (Tecumseh, Shawnee)[298]

There was a time when our forefathers owned this great island. Their seats extended from the rising to the setting sun. The Great Spirit had made it for the use of the Indians. . . . But an evil day came upon us. Your forefathers crossed the great water and landed on this island. Their numbers were small. They found friends and not enemies. They told us they had fled from their own country for fear of wicked men and had come here to enjoy their religion. They asked for a small seat. We took pity on them, granted their request; and they sat down amongst us. We gave them corn and meat, they gave us poison in return.

The white people had now found our country. Tidings were carried back, and more came amongst us. Yet we did not fear them. We took them to be friends. They called us brothers. We believed them, and gave them a larger seat. At length their numbers had greatly increased. They wanted more land; they wanted our country. Our eyes were opened, and our minds became uneasy. Wars took place. Indians were hired to fight against Indians, and many of our

people were destroyed. They also brought strong liquors amongst us.
It was strong and powerful, and has slain thousands. (Red Jacket,
Seneca)[299]

When one man had formerly liberty to purchase lands, and he
took the deed from the Indians for it, and then dies; after his death
his children forge a deed like the true one, with the same Indian
names to it, and thereby take lands from the Indians which they
never sold; this is fraud. Also when one king has land beyond the
river, and another king has land on this side, both bounded by rivers,
mountains and springs which cannot be moved, and the proprie-
taries, greedy to purchase lands, buy of one king what belongs to
another; this likewise is fraud. Yes, I have been served so in this
province; all the land extending from Tohiccon, over the great
mountain, to Wyoming, has been taken from me by fraud; for when
I had agreed to sell land to the old proprietary, by the course of the
river, the young proprietaries came and got it run by a straight
course, by the compass, and by that means took in double the
quantity intended to be sold. (Tadeuskund, Delaware)[300]

We first came to this country a long time ago, and when we sat
ourselves down upon it, we met with a great many hardships and
difficulties. Our country was then very large, but it has dwindled
away to a small spot, and you wish to purchase that! This has caused
us to reflect much upon what you have told us; and we have,
therefore, brought all the chiefs and warriors, and the young men
and women and children of our tribe, that one part may not do what
the others object to, and that all may be witness of what is going
forward. You know your children. Since you first came among
them, they have listened to your words with an attentive ear, and
have always harkened to your counsels. Whenever you had a
proposal to make to us, whenever you have had a favor to ask of us,
we have always lent a favorable ear, and our invariable answer has
been yes. This you know! A long time has passed since we first came
upon our lands, and our old people have all sunk into their graves.
They had sense. We are all young and foolish, and do not wish to do
anything that they would not approve, were they living. We are
fearful we shall offend their spirits, if we sell our lands; and we are
fearful we shall offend you, if we do not sell them. . . . Our country
was given to us by the Great Spirit, who gave it to us to hunt upon,
to make our cornfields upon, to live upon, and to make down our

beds upon when we die . . . and we wish to have some lands for our children to hunt upon. You are gradually taking away our hunting grounds. Your children are driving us before them. . . . I am an Indian, a red-skin, and live by hunting and fishing, but my country is already too small; and I do not know how to bring up my children, if I give it all away. . . . We have now told you what we had to say. It is what was determined on, in a council among ourselves; and what I have spoken, is the voice of my nation. . . . Take pity on us and on our words. (Metea, Potawatomi)[301]

When the white man had warmed himself before the Indian's fire, and filled himself with the Indian's hominy, he became very large; he stopped not for the mountain tops, and his feet covered the plains and the valleys. His hands grasped the eastern and the western sea. Then he [President Jackson] became our great father. He loved his red children; but said, You must move a little farther, lest I should, by accident, tread on you. With one foot he pushed the red man over the Oconee, and with the other he trampled down the graves of his fathers. But our great father still loved his red children, and he soon made them another talk. He said much; but it all meant nothing, but move a little farther; you are too near me. I have heard a great many talks from our great father; and they all began and ended the same. Brothers! When he made us a talk on a former occasion, he said, Get a little farther; go beyond the Oconee and the Oakmulgee; there is a pleasant country. He also said, It shall be yours forever. Now he says, The land you live on is not yours; go beyond the Mississippi; there is game; there you may remain while the grass grows and the water runs. Brothers! Will not our great father come there also? He loves his red children, and his tongue is not forked. (Speckled Snake, Cherokee)[302]

All red men have equal rights to the unoccupied land. The right of occupancy is as good in one place as in another. There cannot be two occupations in the same place. The first excludes all others. It is not so in hunting or traveling; for there the same ground will serve many, as they may follow each other all day; but the camp is stationary, and that is occupancy. It belongs to the first who sits down on his blanket or skins, which he has thrown upon the ground, and till he leaves it no other has a right. (Tecumseh, Shawnee)[303]

I love to roam over the prairies. There I feel free and happy, but when we settle down we grow pale and die. (Satanta, Kiowa)[304]

How come the white man got the country for nothing and now he owes everyone for it? (an old chief, Chippewa)[305]

A party of Sioux Chiefs were being shown the sights of Washington, D.C. After explaining how the white man values works of art as they passed through the Corcoran Art Gallery, the following comment ensued: Ah!, exclaimed an old man, such is the strange philosophy of the white man! He hews down the forest that has stood for centuries in its pride and grandeur, tears up the bosom of mother earth, and causes the silvery watercourses to waste and vanish away. He ruthlessly disfigures God's own pictures and monuments, and then daubs a flat surface with many colors, and praises his work as a masterpiece! (anecdote, Sioux)[306]

The white man likes to pile up stones [construct tall buildings], and he may go to the top of them; I will not. I have ascended the mountains made by Tirawa. (The Kurahus Tahirussawichi, Pawnee)[307]

Why do you believe letters and arts superior to the pursuits of the bow and arrow? Do they more truly fulfill the ambitions of the human heart, according to the measure of light and knowledge, which determine the actual conditions of the different races of men? (Apaumet, Mohican)[308]

The white man thinks with his head—the Indian thinks with his heart. (Ho-chee-nee, Cherokee)[309]

They [my people] were strong and brave and virtuous, according to their knowledge. If they have failed to live up to the standards of the white race, they at least have fought for their own convictions. Who can say that in future generations they will not contribute something of untold value to the life of our nation? Surely strength of character is a commendable trait and our white friends would very well profit by some of our tribal teachings, such as loyalty, perseverance, and self-reliance. (Thomas Wildcat Alford, Shawnee)[310]

Brothers, the Great Spirit has met here with his children of the woods and their pale face brethren. I see his golden locks in the sunshine: he fans the warrior's brows with his wings and whispers sweet music in the winds; the beetle joins his hymn and the mockingbird his song. You are charmed! Brothers, you have been deceived! A snake has been coiled in shade and you are running into his open mouth, deceived by the double tongue of the pale face. (Hopethleycholo, Creek)[311]

Where are the warriors today? Who slew them? Where are our lands? Who owns them?

What white man can say I ever stole his lands or a penny of his money? Yet they say I am a bad Indian. What white man has ever seen me drunk? Who has ever seen me beat my wives or abuse my children? What law have I broken? Is it wrong for me to love my own? Is it wicked in me because my skin is red; because I am a Sioux; because I was born where my fathers lived; because I would die for my people and my country? (Sitting Bull, Hunkpapa Sioux)[312]

You say, Mr. Preacher, that the place I'm going to is a nice place, eh? [A U.S. court sentenced him to die by hanging.]

I'll tell you what I'll do with you. I will give you just twenty-five head of ponies if you will take my place today, as you say it is such a nice place; because I do not like to go right now. (Kintpuash, Modoc)[313]

A cowboy and an Indian die and go to heaven. They get met by St. Peter at the pearly gates, and St. Pete ushers the cowboy into a Cadillac. The angels come out and they line the streets. They start to cheer and the cowboy is driven down between the rows of angels while they stand there applauding and tossing confetti, ticker tape, streamers. The Indian is given an old Model-T that can just barely sputter. By the time the old clinker reaches the parade route, nearly all the angels have gone home.

The Indian is a little upset. I had to take all that abuse on earth, he grumbles. Now when I go to heaven, I get the same treatment. The cowboy is up front in the Cadillac, and I'm in the back in an old Model-T.

St. Peter takes the Indian aside, puts an arm around him, and says, You must understand. We are pleased to have you in heaven; but you see, this is the first cowboy we've ever had! (Dallas Chief Eagle, Lakota)[314]

You who are wise must know, that different nations have different conceptions of things; and you will therefore not take it amiss, if our ideas of this kind of education [at William and Mary College, Williamsburg, Virginia in 1744] happen not to be the same with yours. We had some experience of it: several of our young people were formerly brought up at the colleges of the northern provinces; they were instructed in all your sciences; but when they came back to us, they were bad runners; ignorant of every means of living in the woods; unable to bear either cold or hunger; knew neither how to build a cabin, take a deer, or kill an enemy; spoke our language imperfectly; were therefore neither fit for hunters, warriors, or counsellors; they were totally good for nothing. We are, however, not less obliged by your kind offer, though we decline accepting it; and to show our grateful sense of it, if the gentlemen of Virginia will send us a dozen of their sons, we will take great care of their education, instruct them in all we know, and make men of them. (chief's address in council, Five Nations Iroquois Confederacy)[315]

May the Great Spirit shed light on yours [opinions], and that you may never experience the humiliation that the power of the American Government has reduced me to, is the wish of him who, in his native forests, was once as proud as you. (Black Hawk, Sauk)[316]

As a peace was not concluded on between us at the Rock-landing meeting, your demand for property taken by our warriors from off the disputed lands cannot be admitted. We, also, have had our losses, by captures made by your people. We are willing to conclude a peace with you, but you must not expect extraordinary concessions from us. In order to spare the further effusion of human blood, and to finally determine the war, I am willing to concede, in some measure, if you are disposed to treat on the ground of mutual concession. (Alexander McGillivray, Creek)[317]

We do not stand any show; we cannot talk with these chains on our legs. I feel like I am in a dream, everything is out of my reach, I have nothing to stand on. I cannot say anything that will help any of us. I have lost my day and I know it. (Kintpuash, Modoc)[318]

The United States Government is a strange monster with many heads. One head doesn't know what the others are up to. (John Fire/Lame Deer, Lakota)[319]

A man was chief only as long as he did the will of the people. If he got to be too chiefy, he'd go to sleep one night, and wake up the next morning to find that he was chief all to himself. The tribe would move away in the night, and they didn't wait four years to do it either. (Sun Bear, Chippewa)[320]

A United States Cavalry officer remarked to Spotted Tail that an honest man could be recognized by the hair on his palms and was told in reply: *My friend, I used to have hair on my palms; but shaking hands with so many dishonest white men has worn the hair all off.* (Spotted Tail, Brulé Sioux)[321]

It is customary with us to make a Present of Skins, whenever we renew our Treaties. We are ashamed to offer our Brethren so few, but your Horses and Cows have eaten the Grass our Deer used to feed on. This has made them scarce, and will, we hope, plead in Excuse for our not bringing a larger Quantity. (Canasateego, Onondaga)[322]

We love the white man, but we fear your success. This pretty country you took away from us, but you see how dry it is now. It is only good for red ants, coyotes, and cattlemen. (Quanah Parker, Comanche)[323]

The first subject to which we would call the attention of the governor, is the depredations that are daily committed by the white people upon the most valuable timber on our reservations. This has been a subject of complaint with us for many years; but now, and particularly at this season of the year, it has become an alarming evil, and calls for the immediate interposition of the governor in our behalf. Our next subject of complaint is the frequent thefts of our horses and cattle by the white people, and their habit of taking and using them whenever they please, and without our leave. These are evils which seem to increase upon us with the increase of our white neighbors, and they call loudly for redress. Another evil arising from the pressure of the whites upon us, and our unavoidable communication with them, is the frequency with which our chiefs, and warriors, and Indians, are thrown into jail, and that, too, for the most trifling causes. This is very galling to our feelings, and ought not to be permitted to the extent to which, to gratify their bad passions, our white neighbors now carry this practice. In our hunting and fishing, too, we are greatly interrupted by the whites. Our venison is stolen from the trees where we have hung it to be reclaimed after the chase. Our hunting camps have been fired into, and we have been warned that we shall no longer be permitted to

*pursue the deer in those forests which were so lately all our own.
The fish, which, in the Buffalo and Tonnewanta Creeks, used to supply us with food, are now, by the dams and other obstructions of the
white people, prevented from multiplying, and we are almost entirely deprived of that accustomed sustenance.* (Red Jacket, Seneca)[324]

*To him [the Indian], as to other single-minded men in every age
and race, the love of possessions has appeared a snare, and the
burden of a complex society a source of needless peril and
temptation. . . . To the untutored sage, the concentration of
population was the prolific mother of all evils, moral no less than
physical. He argued that food is good, while surfeit kills; that love is
good, but lust destroys; and no less dreaded than the pestilence
following upon crowded and unsanitary dwellings was the loss of
spiritual power inseparable from too close contact with one's fellowmen.* (Ohiyesa, Santee Sioux)[325]

*The white man builds big house, cost much money, like big
cage, shut out sun, can never move; always sick. Indians and
animals know better how to live than white man; nobody can be in
good health if he does not have all the time fresh air, sunshine and
good water. If the Great Spirit wanted men to stay in one place he
would make the world stand still; but He made it to always change,
so birds and animals can move and always have green grass and ripe
berries, sunlight to work and play, and night to sleep; always
changing; everything for good; nothing for nothing.*

*The white man does not obey the Great Spirit; that is why the
Indians never could agree with him.* (Flying Hawk, Oglala Sioux)[326]

*I live in fear! There is no man I hate, no matter who he is, or
what he is. But I live in fear of the white man. I fear the death he
possesses. I fear the violence that is in him. And I would not be
surprised if one day the white man killed himself, and all of us. I live
in terrible fear of that.*

*The white man hates himself. And he hates the Great Spirit. I
think of that sometimes. Why else would the white man do the
things he does? The things he has done to the Indians? To everyone? I
do not believe that the white man feels guilty, as they say; he is too
full of hate.*

*Can the white man be saved from himself? I wonder. Will he
have to be damned? I wonder. Will he have to go to hell before he
is saved? I wonder.*

The white man's going to hell right now! (Reverend Vine Deloria, Sr., Yankton Sioux)[327]

I feel my country has got a bad name, and I want it to have a good name. It used to have a good name, and I sit sometimes and wonder who it is that has given it a bad name. You [Euro-Americans] are the only people now who can give it a good name, and I want you to take good care of my country and respect it. (Sitting Bull, Hunkpapa Sioux)[328]

Tribe follows tribe, and nation follows nation, like the waves of the sea. It is the order of nature, and regret is useless. Your time of decay may be distant, but will surely come, for even the White Man whose God walked and talked with him as friend with friend, cannot be exempt from the common destiny. (Seattle, Duwamish)[329]

Lifestyle:
The Circle Of Many Points

The history of humankind in America was thousands of centuries old before the arrival of Europeans. It was a land populated by numerous peoples with diverse lifestyles. However, romanticized versions of the morality and courage of eastern pilgrims and western pioneers have anesthetized Euro-Americans to accept preconditioned notions of national history which obscure the moral virtues and fascinating variety of personalities of native Americans who, being the continent's first inhabitants, focalize historical perspective. The problem arises from a human tendency to hold an entire race of people rather than individuals responsible for deeds. This practice leads to erroneous conclusions: Caucasians are industrious and peaceful; all other races are lazy and warlike. Nostalgia perpetuates this view.

Yet, it is individual character, varied by culture and environment which ultimately shapes history and directs human destiny. In their own time, some individuals achieve dignity by serving the common good of society; others dissipate their energies in corrupt pastimes. Not all virtuous men attained greatness, nor are all great men virtuous. The enigma of human nature binds humankind to those who have gone before; but essentially, each one lives by his own beliefs, traditions and social memory unremoved from the natural world, a world humanity had no hand in creating.

Algic

An old one. Pre-Columbian.
This elderly, unidentified tribesman related "The Broken

Wing," a pre-Columbian allegory that was first recorded in English in 1829. It conveyed to those who heard it a lesson of the ways in which members could assure the survival of the tribe by practicing brotherly love, self-denial, consideration for others, gratitude, self-sacrifice, and generosity to the poor and weak.

Apache

Proverb.

Proverbs and adages are time-honored truths which condense the wisdom of experience. These brief expressions lend themselves readily to memorization and instruction in rules of conduct and ethical behavior. Proverbs also illustrate such instructions to bring about a conscientious standard of principles which appeal to the character and real condition of human nature, that is, based on human nature as it is rather than on imagined perception.

Chiricahua Apache

Niño Cochise. 1874 to ?

Niño Cochise exemplified character traits admired by people everywhere: pride in his heritage, perseverance, respectfulness toward his elders, and flexible and philosophical in adversity.

Niño Cochise was born in Arizona Territory, the son of Tahza and Niome (also called Nod-Ah-Sti), the grandson of Chief Cochise, and the nephew of Geronimo. After the U.S. violated an 1872 treaty, Niño, his mother and other clan members, including the shaman Dee-O-Det, fled to the State of Sonora in Mexico. They settled in the Sierra Madre and named their encampment Pa-Gotzin-Kay (Stronghold Mountain of Paradise).

Tahza died in 1876 while attending to tribal business in Washington, D.C.; he was buried in the Congressional Cemetery in a grave that remained unmarked until 1960. The clan then depended on the leadership of Niome and Dee-O-Det until Niño reached the age of fifteen. At that time, he was elected chief and given the emblem of a Thunderbird, the symbol which identified him as the principal chief of the Chiricahui. To carry out his duties, he learned to speak Spanish and English.

Niño, having fled the U.S. in search of freedom, declined an invitation from Theodore Roosevelt to join the "Rough Riders" in America's fight to free Cuba from Spanish domination. Major General Leonard Wood who assisted Roosevelt in recruiting volunteers, was active in later campaigns against Geronimo.

In 1903, Niño left Pa-Gotzin-Kay to work fulltime as bodyguard to a coppermine magnate; it was his first experience in living among white people. The road through the white man's world proved far more difficult and heartbreaking than the rough trails in the Sierra Madre. After the deaths of his mother and Dee-O-Det, who reportedly survived to the age of around 111, Niño went to Hollywood, California, to perform in films starring Douglas Fairbanks, Sr.; Richard Dix; William S. Hart; and the first motion picture with John Wayne. He also worked as a guide for a travel agency, rode in parades as Chief Cochise, and entered into business partnerships. In 1947, at the age of seventy-three, he soloed in an airplane. He piloted his own plane until 1950, when a crash left him seriously injured and permanently disabled.

Niño, who spent his childhood in an earth wickiup, was alive to witness the first landing of men on the moon. In old age, he found that the white man's world, despite its marvels of advanced technology, left much to be desired, and he yearned for the land of his father. He returned to Arizona to open the Cochise Trading Post. At age ninety-six, he was still in business near historic Tombstone, "The town too tough to die."

In 1974, Niño realized a life-long wish to return to the Chiricahua Mountains when he and his wife, Minnie, took title to a new home in Arizona. The property straddles the path leading to the former stronghold of his grandfather, Chief Cochise.

Geronimo. 1829 to 1909.

According to Geronimo's autobiography, the Bedonkohe band to which he belonged was encamped in Arizona's Nodoyohn Canyon at the time of his birth in 1829. However, some historians theorize that Geronimo was born near old Ft. Tulerosa, New Mexico. Taklishim (The Gray One) and Juana called their son Goyathlay (One Who Yawns). Taklishim died when Geronimo was still a youth; because his mother never remarried, he assumed responsibility for her care.

At age seventeen, he joined a band of warriors led by Mangas

Coloradas (Red Sleeves). It was during this period in his life that Geronimo's mother, wife, and three children were wantonly killed by Mexican troops. The tragedy resulted in a lifelong pursuit for revenge and a reckless live-or-die attitude in battle.

He was sociable, and even a single listener animated him to tell humorous anecdotes about himself and others, plus to relate spellbinding accounts of his experiences. There was about him that mystique which surrounds adventurous men, and he never failed to capture the attention of an audience. His presence created a feeling of tension and a desire for action. Geronimo was a persuasive speaker with a very creative mind. He could devise cunning schemes that others found so appealing that they would be enticed to organize a fight or raid. Numerous followers and admirers idolized him.

Geronimo was a medicine man as well as a war chief. Contemporaries said he had an uncanny sixth sense and a prescient mind to guide him. He obviously led a charmed life to survive the fifty bullet wounds which scarred his body. He himself was an expert marksman.

Frustrated by the lack of stimulation from spontaneous challenges, Geronimo deplored his confinement at San Carlos, Arizona; people called it "Hell's Forty Acres." Fluent in Spanish, Geronimo escaped to Mexico several times between 1876 and 1886. To avoid capture, acts of daring—even half-savage ones—were necessary to anticipate and outwit his uncompromising adversary, the U.S. Cavalry. Until his voluntary return, Geronimo, of all Indians, was last to accept the dominant society's moral and geographical boundaries. He was confined in prison, but after his release, he settled at Ft. Sill in the Oklahoma Territory. There, he joined the Dutch Reformed Church and became a Sunday-school teacher.

At the St. Louis World's Fair in 1904, Geronimo appeared in roping contests and sold his photographs. Each picture retailed for twenty-five cents, but the Bureau of Indian Affairs allowed him to keep only ten cents. Geronimo boosted his income by charging ten to twenty-five cents more to autograph them and was permitted to keep all the money from this source. In 1905, he was invited to Theodore Roosevelt's inaugural parade. Geronimo was a very popular attraction at the World's Fair in Omaha, Nebraska, where he did a brisk business in handmade miniature bows and arrows and other souvenir items.

Geronimo's need to exercise his mind did not diminish as he neared his eightieth birthday. Giving his imagination free reign, he contrived situations that produced the desired activity. He supplemented his income by sitting for artists and photographers. When paid for his time, he consented to interviews by writers seeking his viewpoint on historical incidents. A large share of his income was sent to needy families at San Carlos.

The warrior chief's life ended in 1909 at the Ft. Sill post hospital. The fort is now a historical site and one of its major "attractions" is the Geronimo Guardhouse. Geronimo's grave is on the East Range of the Wichita Mountains, having allegedly been moved from the cemetery near Ft. Sill.

Jicarilla Apache

Ancient ethic. *See* Omaha, moral teaching.

Mescalero Apache

Chris. 1880 to ?

His Indian name was In The Middle. His mother, Compra, was related to Chief Peso. The family of his father, Hide The Moccasin, was prominent among the Chiricahui. Chris, born about 1880, was almost six years old when federal authorities isolated Chiricahua men from the women and children. He and his mother were sent as prisoners of war to Florida and, later, Alabama. In 1889, Chris and his mother were settled on the Mescalero Apache Reservation in New Mexico, but it was not until 1913 that the tribe was released from its prisoner-of-war status.

Chris attended schools in Albuquerque and Santa Fe. Congenial, he easily acquired friends among tribesmen and Euro-Americans. His practice of Apache religious tenets—including belief in the existence of paratypical powers—made him a prime informant when anthropologists recorded tribal customs. He was a skilled hunter and an acknowledged expert in plant and animal identification. Because of his work with naturalists and his extraordinary memory, Chris learned the scientific names of a large variety of birds and animals inhabiting the reservation area.

For a time, Chris was a reservation policeman, but more as a duty in taking his turn at the chore than from desire or interest in the work. He became a cattle rancher, and in 1908 married the daughter of Mescalero leader Muchacho Negro.

Impelled by insatiable curiosity, Chris was especially fascinated by curing rites, ceremonials and songs which he rendered in a pleasant voice. He was analytical in discerning the secret herbs used by a shaman. His father, mother and a maternal aunt were widely sought as practicing medicine doctors.

Hide The Moccasin made the war bonnet that was part of the Indian collection of The American Museum of Natural History.

Mimbres Apache

Victorio. 1820 to 1880.

Two countries proclaim themselves the birthplace of Victorio: the U.S. and Mexico. Apaches say that he was born around 1820 in New Mexico and was a Chiricahua by birth. Tribesmen of the Chihennes band, to which he belonged, knew him by the name Bidu-ya. Across the border, he is proudly identified as a Mexican child-captive seized by the Apache during a raid on Hacienda del Carmen in the State of Chihuahua. In either event, he did grow up in the U.S. but lived in Mexico at a later age. Victorio had a son called Washington, and a sister, Lozen, a famous clairvoyant. Victorio's people were referred to as "Coppermine Apache" because the legendary Santa Rita coppermines of New Mexico lay within their territory.

Victorio was a close friend of Cochise and Mangas Coloradas. The trio, when banded together, were an awesome sight that brought fear to their enemies and a thrill of pride to their allies. Cochise was six feet tall, well muscled and very strong. Soldiers called him "The Serpent" for his skill on the battlefield. Mangas Coloradas was six feet five inches tall, and had a sinewy, athletic physique. Victorio was almost six feet tall; lithe, quick movements marked him a man of action with tremendous reserves of energy.

Between 1862 and 1871, they almost succeeded in reclaiming Arizona from the Euro-Americans. However, the tribe suffered severe deprivation after white traders decimated the buffalo herds. Victorio agreed to lead his Ajo Caliente band to a New Mexico reservation located on ancestral land. But events write their own rules to which men can only react; Victorio typifies the Indians' role in the white man's reign of terror. He considered it the final unendurable outrage in 1877 when the reservation was opened to white settlers and the Apache were scheduled for removal to San Carlos Reservation in Arizona.

The San Carlos Reservation was a desolate place. Vegetation was scarce in the almost continuously hot, dry climate. Abrasive dust-burdened winds stripped the plains bare of growth; swarms of insects infested the area; provisions were inadequate to support the multitude of Apaches crowded onto the parcel of land set aside for their use. Victorio resisted the removal, and a series of escapes and recaptures dominated the years that followed.

Victorio opted for a chance at freedom and peace in Mexico, and the Apache exodus thus began in 1880. The journey was made more arduous by pursuing U.S. armed forces because it necessitated frequent stops to build rock defenses—a trademark of Victorio's battles.

Successful in reaching Mexico, Victorio encamped in Miguel Canyon. But the unfettered life he had envisioned was quickly dispelled by political machinations, which ever tend to crush the dreams of the less powerful. Disputes between the U.S. and Mexico focused on the Apache as a cause of contention. Whenever the U.S. military ended its pursuit at the border, the Apache were soon hunted in turn by Mexican troops.

In a surprise attack at Tres Castillos in 1880, Victorio was surrounded by Mexican soldiers before he could move his men to a more advantageous position. Few Apaches survived; one who did not, was Victorio. Apaches say that he fought until he ran out of ammunition and then committed suicide to avoid capture.

However, Euro-Americans and Mexicans credit Mauricio Corredor with slaying Victorio. For this "magnificent" deed, he received many fine gifts, including a nickle-plated rifle, which, according to some accounts, was used to kill U.S. Army Captain Emmet Crawford. At the time, Crawford was pursuing Geronimo and stopped to rest his troops in the Sierra Madre when he was besieged by Mexicans. The gift, given with jubilation upon the death of Victorio, became the instrument which horrified the white society when it heard of Crawford's death.

The man Euro-Americans would not honor in life, they now honor in death. In the Black Range—formerly called Mimbres Mountains—north of Kingston, New Mexico, a peak rising more than ten thousand feet is named for Victorio.

Western Apache

An elderly Apache. *See* Oglala Sioux, village elder.

Anonymous. *See* Eskimo, anonymous.

Tribe member. *See* Omaha, moral teaching.

White Mountain Apache

Diablo. 1840 to late 1880s.
 The White Mountain Apache called him Eskinela and Hacke Ldasila (Angry Right Side Up); Euro-Americans and Mexicans called him Diablo. He was born around 1840 near Turkey Creek in Arizona and was groomed from early childhood to assume the duties of a leader; playmates with whom he hunted rabbit referred to him as "chief." He was known for fearless ventures and for the many wounds he sustained yet survived. The Eastern White Mountain, largest Apache division occupying the Sierra Blanca Mountains region in Arizona, elected him head chief during the decade when they had their first contact with U.S. Government officials—around 1852.
 Diablo was a vigilant observer of the white man's activities in Arizona Territory. After hearing rumors from many sources about a conspiracy planned by whites against native Americans, Diablo cautioned his band to refrain from traveling to Goodwin Springs for rations. His timely advice is credited with sparing the people the grief that befell others who were issued what was suspected by witnesses to have been poisoned meat; many native Americans died on their return journey from Goodwin Springs. The people still sing a song which commemorates the disastrous incident.
 Diablo represented the White Mountain Apache in a peace council held at Ft. Goodwin in 1864. In 1867, his band allowed the U.S. to construct a road from Ft. Goodwin to Whiteriver, Arizona, where another military post, Ft. Apache, was erected.

Ironically, Ft. Apache became another reservation to confine the tribe.

Diablo died during the late 1800s.

Arapaho

Carl Sweezy. 1881 to 1953.

Carl Sweezy was born in a tipi on the Arapaho Reservation near Darlington, Oklahoma. As a child, he was named Wattan (Black). His father was Hinan Ba Seth (Big Man) whose wife died when Wattan was still very young. He was sent to mission schools for his elementary education, and afterwards to high school in Halstead, Kansas. At this time, he began using Carl Sweezy as his name. To bridge the differences between his own and white culture, he adopted an amalgam of what he discerned to be the best in both.

Early in life, Sweezy showed a talent for art and sketched for his own amusement. His career as a professional artist began with a commission in 1900 when he was living in Washington Crossing, Oklahoma. For the next ten years, he recorded the Indian way of life on canvas. His works are delicate and uncluttered; the colors are soft and diffused.

Sweezy sold paintings to private collectors and museums, plus added to his income by dairy farming. He also played with a baseball team headquartered in Enid, Oklahoma, and another team composed entirely of native Americans. During one cross-country tour, he and his teammates visited the Lewis and Clark Exposition in Portland, Oregon. Sweezy was surprised to find his paintings on display as part of an exhibit sponsored by the Smithsonian Institution.

Still athletically lean and virile at age forty, he nevertheless abandoned most activities to devote more time to painting. The increased demand for his art paralleled his growing reputation among admirers who appreciated his self-imposed concern for accuracy and detail.

Sweezy fathered three children after his marriage to Hattie Powless, an Oneida woman who predeceased him in 1944. The Arapaho artist whose home was in Oklahoma City, died in Lawton, Oklahoma in 1953.

Arikara

White Shield. Flourished 1800s.

His chieftainship was hereditary, for such was the custom among the Arikara. There were one hundred eighty warriors in White Shield's camp, but being a proponent of peace, he took up arms only in self-defense or for a just cause. He was an impassioned speaker, but when others spoke in council, he listened with an expression of silent gravity. White Shield participated in many peace parleys and witnessed the steady erosion of tribal territory with much regret. However, he was an ethical man who could be relied on to uphold any treaty sanctioned by the people.

When the Arikara were being relocated to old Ft. Berthold, North Dakota, Federal agents met with the tribe near the Mussel Shell River in Montana and designated Bear Chief as principal chief. Thereby, usurping the people's right to elect their leaders. Bear Chief outwitted the agents by choosing White Shield for a position of equal power in managing tribal affairs.

The Arikara were strong-featured people, proud in manner and appearance, excellent warriors who served with distinction as U.S. Army scouts. White Shield was in charge of an all-native-American police force employed by the Federal government. He was courteous and thoughtful, remembering always to extend condolences when any cavalry troops were killed in combat.

White Shield was very advanced in age in 1867 when it was his misfortune to contend with the thievery of Indian Bureau agents who sold provisions intended for the tribe. The chief had to beg for corn to relieve the people's distress in 1868. White Shield continued in service to the people even into 1875.

Long after his death, White Shield was still esteemed by the Arikara, and in 1941 they erected a concrete monument to mark his grave near Ft. Berthold.

Assiniboine

Fire Bear. Flourished 1900s.

William Standing was his legal name, but as a child he was called Looks In The Clouds. Upon reaching manhood, he adopted the name of his grandfather, Fire Bear, and that was the name he preferred to be known by. His father, Standing Rattle, belonged to the Rock Mountain People band; he was a medicine man and sponsor of the annual Medicine Lodge Dance.

Fire Bear was a descendant of In The Light and Lance, a maternal uncle noted as a painter of medicine lodges—a profession requiring imagination and an extensive knowledge of symbolism.

Fire Bear attended schools near Oswego, Montana (at Wolf Point), and Haskell Institute in Kansas. From a very early age, art provided him with a medium for self-expression. He was known to have a witty humor, but his paintings were earnest. His attention to minute details can be seen in his illustrations of the legends compiled by First Boy. At age seventy-six, Standing Rattle was the principal source of these accounts which originated with ancestors living one hundred fifty years ago and passed down through the families of the informants. Fire Bear closely questioned each tribesman for essential features of dress and utensils to create authentic portrayals in his paintings.

Fire Bear's paintings have been exhibited at the Washington, D.C. Art Club—at the time Charles Curtis, a part Kaw Indian was Vice President of the U.S.—and in various states. His work was also displayed at the Colonial Art Exhibit in Paris, France. Fire Bear died prior to 1960 and did not see the published book he illustrated about the Assiniboine.

First Boy. 1888 to ?

James Larpenteur Long, or First Boy, was born in 1888 in a village near present-day Oswego, Montana. His father, who died before his son's birth, was a government employee assigned to teach farming techniques to the Assiniboine. First Boy was raised according to ancient customs by his mother, Annie, and his maternal grandmother, Makes Cloud Woman, daughter of Chief First Fly of the Rock People Band.

At age seven, he entered Poplar River Boarding School, returning home for summer vacations to hunt with bow and arrow, and later with rifle. He was ten years old when he was named First Boy to signify that he was "a leader among boys." At the same time, to commemorate an important event in the tribe's history, the additional names Almost Killed, Swims About and

Comes Back Alive were bestowed upon him. He was twelve when he was initiated into the secret Horse Society.

Annie and Makes Cloud Woman were converted to Catholicism, and First Boy was baptized in 1896. He attended school to the age of seventeen and found employment as a clerk for a trading company. From 1913 to 1919, he was a cattle-and-horse rancher. But after his wife's death, he sold the livestock and returned to Oswego to clerk in his father-in-law's store, which he and a partner purchased in later years. Around 1938, he opened a grocery store on his own in Oswego where he still lived in 1960.

Tribesmen congregated there, passing the time by telling stories heard from old ones and of their own experiences. First Boy compiled and published these tales and others obtained by interviewing the oldest living tribe members, one being over one hundred years old.

First Boy's tribal activities included membership on the Executive Board of the Tribal Council, the 1851 Treaty Committee, secretary for resettlement of Indian families on an experimental irrigation unit and Director of the Fort Peck United Projects—to promote irrigation, power and national defense plans for the Fort Peck Dam.

First Boy had extensive knowledge of Indian lore. He could write and speak the Assiniboine language and several dialects fluently. His skill in sign language was used to interview old informants who were hearing impaired.

Ochankugahe. 1874 to ?

His name means Pathmaker, it was given to him by his grandfather, Panapin, to honor the elderly man's success in leading tribesmen through a winter blizzard across the vast plains of Saskatchewan. Ochankugahe was born in 1874 and grew up at Cypress Hills, Canada.

The tribe was moved to the Assiniboine Reserve at Skull Mountainettes in 1882 where they shared the land with a band that was half Assiniboine and half Cree. This band's leader was Chief Payepot.

At age twelve, Ochankugahe entered school in Lebret where he was given his first short haircut and a new name, Dan Kennedy. He continued his education and earned a degree from

St. Boniface College in Manitoba. In 1895, he accompanied Chief Payepot to the first Territorial Exhibition held in Regina.

Ochankugahe crossed the U.S.-Canadian border many times to visit relatives living at Wolf Point and on the Ft. Belknap Reservation in Montana. In 1936, he joined a research expedition to Standing Rock Agency in the Dakotas. His written works reveal a literate man, intelligent and thorough in telling the history of his people with sympathy and understanding as he and they experienced it.

Social tradition. *See* Omaha, moral teaching.

Traditional grandfather's advice. *See* Oglala Sioux, village elder.

Tribal code. *See* Omaha, moral teaching.

Tribal sage. *See* Oglala Sioux, village elder.

Blackfoot

Crowfoot. 1826 to 1890.

During his childhood, he was called Shot Close (Astoxkom) and Bear Ghost (Kyiahstaah), but he is best known as Crowfoot (Sapo Omarxika). Around 1826, he was born in a village on Bow River to a Blood tribe mother and Blackfoot chief, The Many Names, whom Crowfoot succeeded.

He participated in his first war exploit at the age of thirteen, but in later years, because of his tact and strength of character, he was frequently called on to act as a peacemaker; he traveled often between the United States and Canada. Sitting Bull, during his sojourn at Cypress Hills in Canada, conferred with Crowfoot in an unsuccessful attempt to persuade him to unite their tribes in a pact of mutual assistance.

White Calf. 1825 to 1905.

At the time of White Calf's birth, around 1825, the Blackfoot tribe still hunted bison between the Yellowstone and North Saskatchewan rivers in the Great Plains region that stretches from Central Saskatchewan to Texas. A free man who gloried in his liberty, White Calf roamed the Great Plains for more than sixty years, sometimes venturing as far south as Mexico. When he was over seventy years old, there was still an aura of energetic alertness to his high-spirited movements and his erect posture on horseback. But his land and his freedom shrank in direct proportion to the burgeoning horde of settlers who came. Overwhelmed by the dominant society, and fearing needless loss of life without hope of success, White Calf advised the people to adapt to the changes imposed by white culture. Some of the tribe now live on reserves in Alberta and Saskatchewan, Canada. Others, like White Calf, settled on the Blackfoot Reservation in Montana.

With his wife, Catches Two Horses, Chief White Calf chose a parcel of land along Cut Bank Creek, not far from Browning. Diligent and conscientious in attending to the tribe's welfare, he exercised discerning judgment and was paternalistic and benevolent in carrying out his duties. White Calf was especially generous to orphans, widows, and the poor. The people appreciated his kindness and for almost thirty years the Blackfoot retained him as their principal chief.

White Calf was guardian of the Beaver Bundle, and with his wife co-sponsored a Sun Dance in 1897 for Mad Wolf. His long years of service came to an end in 1905 when he died at the age of eighty.

Cherokee

A young chief, c. 1735. *See* Eskimo, anonymous.

Ethic.

Peace within family and tribe depended on a conscious effort by each individual to promote harmony. To the extent that their way of life permitted, the women and children led sheltered lives. Social order was a paramount requisite to survival of the tribe, and any disturbance to the tranquility and tempo of daily activities was frowned upon.

Ginaly-li. Flourished mid-1800s and 1900s.

Ginaly-li was immersed in the supernatural. His language was allegory and symbolism with which he conveyed the inner journey through the cosmological world that he experienced as a mystic. An objective study of mysticism is precluded by the very nature of the subject, so we must rely on the personal accounts of mystics themselves.

Ginaly-li, typically intense and zealous in his concern for the good of others, spent long periods in contemplation and fasting. Through introspection, he traveled mystical pathways that led to wisdom and illumination. In the late years of his life, he expressed with humility his gratitude for having been blessed with insight into the mysteries that helped him to realize his direct relationship with the all-encompassing Life-Force.

Perceiving the changes superimposed by white culture upon his own, Ginaly-li tried to understand and explain them in the context of traditions set down by the Ancient Ones.

Ho-chee-nee. 1910 to ____.

Her name means "The Leader." She is also known as Jimalee Burton—artist, writer, musician, lecturer. Ho-chee-nee was born at Elreno, Oklahoma in 1910. She earned her college credits at Tulsa University (1940 to 1943), and Oklahoma State Teachers College. Her paintings have won thirty-two ribbons at Oklahoma State fairs. The American Pen Women awarded her its first prize in 1963.

Huey P. Long. Contemporary.

Airman Long lives in Georgia, ancestral residence of the Cherokee. The interest in aviation which preoccupied him at an early age led to his becoming a Civil Air Patrol cadet when he was still in high school. He has since obtained a pilot's license, having served with a fighter wing unit of the Georgia Air National Guard. He is an Air Force reservist and in 1976 was assigned to a base in Georgia as a recreational specialist. Airman Long was program planner and administrator of the gymnasium serving personnel of the Air Force Reserve, Air National Guard, Army Guard, Naval Air Reserve and Marine Air Reserve.

Huey P. Long graduated from the University of Georgia with a degree in business administration.

John Ross. 1790 to 1866.

The child born to Scotsman Daniel Ross and Mary McDonald, a Cherokee, in 1790 near the Coosa River in Georgia was called Little John (Tsan-usdi). John Ross belonged to the Bird

Clan, and in later years was known as Coowescoowe (Egret) or Guwisgu (Swan).

Educated in Kingston, Tennessee schools, he was commissioned an officer at age twenty-three, serving under General Andrew Jackson in the Creek–American War of 1813 to 1814. Ross mingled with and dressed in the style fashionable among Euro-Americans, gaining steadily a reputation for leadership in both Indian and white communities. After the Cherokee adopted their first written constitution in 1827, Ross was sworn in as principal chief at the nation's General Council in 1828.

Ross was living in Tennessee when the Georgia Guard crossed state lines in 1835 to illegally arrest and confine him in prison. Shortly thereafter, the Georgia militia suppressed publication of the *Cherokee Phoenix*, the Cherokee nation's central news outlet.

When gold was discovered on tribal land, Euro-Americans began a campaign to dispossess the Cherokee. Ross fought against the removal but was unable to withstand the gold-seeking squatters. To assure humane treatment, Ross supervised the removal of almost thirteen thousand Cherokee in a single month. Thousands of people died on the trail; one of them was Ross' wife, Elizabeth Brown Henley or Quatie (First One). She was buried beside the road at Little Rock, Arkansas, on February 1, 1839. Among the Cherokee, the removal to Indian Territory is referred to as Numadautsuny (The Trail Where They Cried); others call it the Trail of Tears.

Settled at Park Hill, the reunited Cherokee again elected Ross to be their principal chief; he retained the position until his death in 1866. Ross was an ardent gardener and was especially fond of cultivating roses; he called his farm Rose Cottage.

The tribe prospered and fifteen years after arriving at Park Hill, Ross attended public functions in a glistening coach with a driver and footman. This was not a pretentious display, for Ross was a good, kind and humble man. Dependable transportation was a necessity because he traveled extensively on tribal business. Ross was always available to his people and they felt at ease when coming to him with a problem at any hour of the day or night. Ross was in Washington, D.C., on behalf of the Cherokee when he died, but he was buried in Park Hill.

A reenactment of the Trail of Tears is performed each year at Tsa-la-gi in Tahlequah, Oklahoma.

Speckled Snake. Flourished 1800s.

He was chief of a Cherokee band and a contemporary of John Ross. Speckled Snake was sophisticated and cognizant of the devious and intricate political maneuverings of government authorities, and he dealt with them on intellectually equal terms. However, he could not match the arms and manpower of his adversaries.

Unlike modern times when governments have shown a greater social conscience toward native American rights—the New York State–Seneca agreement in 1976, and the court awarded compensation in 1979 to the Sioux for the Black Hills confiscation are examples—the dominant society of earlier years did not question its right to appropriate land with or without legal process.

Lust for the gold on tribal property created so much agitation that a design to forcefully remove the Cherokee brought about a period of oppression and travail for the Cherokee nation. The size of the gold deposit whetted men's imaginations, and the energy they expended to gain possession of it was boundless. It was worth more than one hundred million dollars; the ore deposit ran for almost one hundred miles on a straight line southward towards the western corner of Carroll County, and continued in a single bed estimated to be about thirty miles wide in its southern portion.

Not even the cogent debates of Speckled Snake could stem the onslaught of whites in pursuit of this wealth.

Tsali. ? to 1838.

Tsali was a leader of the Ani Keetoowah; his family traced its ancestry to the oldest of the Keetoowah Cherokee blood lines. White settlers, finding it difficult to pronounce his name, called him "Charley" or "Dutch." With his wife, Amanda, and a young son, aging Tsali lived in a log house high up in the Great Smoky Mountains of Georgia. His two adult sons and their families also farmed in the hill country during the early 1800s.

Cherokee territory abounded in fertile plains through which vast herds of cattle and horses roamed; flocks of sheep, goats, and swine lined the hillsides. There were public roads and taverns with comfortable accommodations for travelers. The tribe harvested crops of corn, cotton, tobacco, wheat, oats, indigo, sweet and Irish potatoes; and butter and cheese were common. They spun cotton and wool, weaving it into cloth on looms built by the men. The Cherokee engaged in commerce without an intermediary government agent. Navigating the waterways, they traded at local towns, and in 1825 began to export cotton to New Orleans in their own vessels. They purchased Black slaves from Euro-Americans, to work their farms, but unlike white slavemasters, the Cherokee maintained an employer-employee relationship.

The people labored long and hard, but they loved the land and their self-sustained independence. On occasion, the Cherokee paid for purchases with gold; these transactions did not go unnoticed in the white community. Once again, gold, the Indians' nemesis and the white man's love, brought into motion a calamitous removal for the sake of "progress."

Tsali, his sons and their families were seized in their homes in 1838 by a deputation of armed soldiers. Forced to abandon all of their possessions, the families were escorted under threat of death to a holding compound at Bushnell, North Carolina, one of several stockades built by the U.S. Army to confine the Cherokee until they could be moved to Indian Territory. Tsali did not resist the soldiers, but brooded over his misfortune as the distance increased from his beloved home.

The military guards, rushing the families along the rough terrain, caused Tsali's elderly wife to stumble; a soldier insensitively prodded her with his bayonet. Tsali found release for his pent-up emotions by devising a plan of escape. He decided upon a simple ruse: he would deliberately stumble and pretend he injured an ankle. With the soldiers off-guard, they could be quickly subdued and disarmed. The plan was followed, but as Tsali grappled with his opponent, the military man's rifle fired accidentally, killing the soldier instantly. Filled with remorse and fear, Tsali led his family to Clingman's Dome, one of the highest mountains in the Great Smokies, where they lived in a cave and subsisted on forest products and small game during the summer and fall.

Tsali, his son Ridges, and his brother-in-law Lowney were pursued as fugitives by armed troops. The three men were asked to surrender and stand trial. In return, the military agreed to cease tracking-down those Cherokee who had either escaped from or evaded captivity. The men knew they were being asked to forfeit their lives so that other Cherokee could live in peace and freedom.

Tsali, Ridges, and Lowney surrendered and were brought before a military court which sentenced them to death by a firing squad at Bushnell in 1838. Their graves lie hidden beneath the waters of Fontana Lake in North Carolina. Because of Tsali's heroic sacrifice, his legend is told as an example of devotion, loyalty, and courage. It has remained an important feature of Cherokee history to the present time.

Cheyenne

Fire Dog. *See* Cheyenne, Hyemeyohsts Storm.

Hyemeyohsts Storm. Contemporary.

Storm's father was a shieldmaker and tutored his son in the art. It was the most magnificent gift he could give, one that had been passed on for many generations. It had been given to the family by the Medicine Powers. Through them, Miaheyyun, the giver of total understanding, bestowed the precious gift upon the people. The language of the shields is also the language of the Medicine Wheel and of the people and their lifeway. It is the Sun Dance, the brotherhood societies, the teachings of the Peace Chiefs, and The Way to self-realization. The significance of the forty-four Great Shields of the Men of Peace, like sign language, is understood by all tribes. Shieldmakers were revered holy men, welcomed wherever they traveled.

Storm teaches through symbolism and allegory in the tradition of the Ancient Ones, the Prophets, the Wise Men— those who have experienced illumination. He successfully transcends the three dimensional world to interpret native American metaphysics in which everything is possible and nothing is improbable, where time does not intrude and oneness prevails in a multitude of reflected images.

In his book, *Seven Arrows,* the figurative characters Fire Dog,
Hawk, Shining Arrows and White Wolf are one yet many; they
are old and yet young; they are of one tribe and all tribes; they are
Everyman.

Like the throb of a long distance drum, Storm creates a
rhythm that weaves a hypnotic charm as he explains the meaning
of the Shields and the Medicine Wheel to recreate and reveal the
heart, mind and soul of the Indian.

Sweet Medicine. Ancient.

Tradition states that this legendary hero was born of a virgin
and blessed with spiritual power. Mutsoyef, as he was called, was
a handsome young man, with mystic ways, who undertook a
pilgrimage to the home of the Holy Ones in the sacred mountain
near Sturgis, South Dakota. The Teton Dakota (Western Sioux)
call the mountain Bear Butte; the Cheyenne call it Nowahwus
(The Hill Where The People Are Taught); it is also known as Pipe
Mountain.

From Miaheyyun, the supreme deity, Sweet Medicine
received four sacred arrows which symbolized the collective tribal
soul, and instructions for performing the rite of Renewal of the
Sacred Arrows. These are the arrows of the Four Directions, the
great powers of the Medicine Wheel that lead to self-fulfillment.
The arrow of the North is the path of Wisdom; the arrow of the
East symbolizes the path of Illumination; the South is the path of
Innocence; and the West is the symbolic path to Introspection.
These are the paths by which man learns about the universe, the
world, his fellowmen and himself. Cheyenne refer to the Sacred
Arrows as the "Ark of the Cheyenne people," because they
represent the continuing unity of the tribe with Miaheyyun.

After receiving the arrows, the prophet was called either
Sweet Medicine or by one of his alternate names, Rustling Corn
Leaf or Sweet Root Standing.

It is said that Sweet Medicine died near the tall rock out-
cropping known as Devil's Tower in Wyoming; others say his
death occurred in the area of Bear Butte. Shortly before his death,
Sweet Medicine's final prophesy foretold the coming of white
strangers with horses and of the subjugation of the people, with a
concurrent loss of their culture.

The successors of Sweet Medicine were men who lived to peaceful old age with few exceptions, just as Sweet Medicine is said to have lived beyond the normal life expectancy.

White Antelope. 1789 to 1864.

Chief White Antelope had many contacts with whites since his birth in 1789, some satisfactory and others unfortunate. He was present at the Ft. Laramie (Wyoming) Treaty Council in 1851, and had been to Washington, D.C., where he was given a Peace Medal as a token of the government's good intentions and esteem. White Antelope was friendly to Euro-Americans although his experience with them proved repeatedly that they were unworthy of his trust. Nevertheless, in good faith, he joined his brother Black Kettle, principal chief of the Southern Cheyenne, and Arapaho Chief Left Hand in accepting an invitation to conclude an armistice at Denver, Colorado.

On arrival they were sent to nearby Ft. Lyon and treated as prisoners of war. Provisions at the fort were inadequate and the captives began to suffer from hunger. Ft. Lyon authorities, after assuring the chiefs of military protection, instructed the unarmed tribes to camp about thirty miles away at Sand Creek to hunt for their own food.

Before long, the encamped Indians were gripped with foreboding when they observed the approach of more than eight hundred troops and four cannons. The United States flag with a white flag beneath it was immediately raised to the top of Black Kettle's lodge. Nevertheless, the cavalry force aimed its weapons at the camp and fired directly at the people and their tipis.

The slaughter raged unabated for more than two hours before the unbridled hate and frenzy of the military was sated. The soldiers, urged by their commanding officer, Colonel John M. Chivington, to "kill and scalp all, big and little," committed acts of extreme barbarity. Kit Carson referred to Chivington, a former Methodist minister, and his men as "cowards and dogs."

In that year, 1864, beneath a white flag, the defenseless and aged White Antelope sang his death song while the military massacred the people. He was shot and scalped. His nose, ear, and genitals were cut off, to make "a tobacco bag out of" them. Three-fourths of the dead were women, children and the elderly.

Wooden Leg. 1858 to 1940.

Long before Wooden Leg's birth in 1858 in a village by the Cheyenne River in the Black Hills of South Dakota, the men of his family were famed for bravery and reliability. His grandfather, No Braids, was delegated to Washington, D.C., on tribal business. Wooden Leg's father was Many Bullet Wounds; his mother was Eagle Feather On The Forehead; they named their son Eats From The Hand. When the boy was fourteen years old, he was invited to join the Elk Scraper Society of which his father and two brothers were already members; only the strong, trustworthy and courageous could belong to the organization. The society was entrusted with guarding the Mahuts (Sacred Arrows).

In search of adventure, Wooden Leg spent long hours and sometimes days roaming the countryside, thereby acquiring a reputation for being a tireless walker. Because of this, at the age of seventeen he was given the name of his much-admired uncle, Wooden Leg.

Wooden Leg was six feet two inches tall and a bit of a dandy with an engaging sense of humor. He spent many hours arranging his hair and clothing in preparation for a social outing and endured a great deal of good-natured teasing because of it. He delighted in dancing and relished the attention he got from admiring girls.

On June 25, 1876, after dancing until dawn, Wooden Leg was aroused from sleep shortly after retiring. The camp was besieged by U.S. Cavalry forces. Wooden Leg arose quickly, but out of habit began to dress with great care. He had to be cajoled into hurrying before he realized the urgency for repelling the attack. Wooden Leg then sped swiftly to the battlefield on the Little Big Horn River where he won much honor that day. The significance of the native Americans' victory in annihilating General George A. Custer and five companies of his Seventh Cavalry unit is still debated by historians.

Wooden Leg was a man of uncommon good sense with a penchant for honesty and truthfulness. Therefore, he represented the Northern Cheyenne at a meeting with authorities in Washington, D.C. At age fifty, he was baptized at the Tongue River mission in Montana, but continued to worship in solitude as had been his custom.

Wooden Leg was fluent in the Sioux language and his own Cheyenne, but used a combination of sign language and a few English words, supplemented with occasional pencil drawings and sketched maps to dictate his autobiography at the age of seventy-three. He lived in Montana until his death in 1940.

Northern Cheyenne

Ancient proverb. *See* Apache, proverb.

Chippewa

An old chief. *See* Oglala Sioux, village elder.

Ted D. Mahto. Contemporary.
Ted Mahto is a poet, writer, lecturer, educator and U.S. armed forces veteran. He was born on the Red Lake Reservation in Minnesota, and has taught German, English, mathematics and physics in reservation schools and in white communities.

His wide-ranging interests include invention of a school curriculum that relates the learning process of native American children to their ethnic background. Mahto foresees an innovative approach which includes visual expression of thought. He says that daydreaming is visual thinking. His ideas define a system of instruction that is gaining acceptance among educators and psychologists. Daydreaming, or stream-of-consciousness, is triggered by external stimuli such as the configuration of a stone, bird song, or the color of a flower. It enriches our capacity for creativity and adds to our personal growth; daydreaming patterns have been observed in children fantacizing during playtime. The native American's psyche has always been finely attuned to stimulation from the observable environment and readily lends itself to creative motivation in education along the concepts envisioned by Mahto.

He also devotes much time to evaluating the theory of Carl Jung's collective unconscious. Mahto surmises that the myths and legends of native Americans are links in, or perhaps the keys to, understanding philosophical and metaphysical truths.

Sun Bear, Contemporary.

Sun Bear was born in northern Minnesota where he grew up on the White Earth Reservation. After reaching his eighteenth birthday, he left the reservation to travel, visiting and studying with native Americans still practicing traditional customs. He has taught at the University of California at Davis and was associated with the Inter-Tribal Council of Nevada.

During his ten years in Hollywood, California, Sun Bear was an actor and technical director for the *Brave Eagle* and *Broken Arrow* television shows. His film roles included portrayal of a Chinaman in *The Ugly American* and a Tibetan in *Marriage-Go-Round.*

Sun Bear organized the Bear Tribe Self-Reliance Center in 1970; membership is open to Euro-Americans as well as native Americans. Located near Spokane, Washington, the Center focuses its activities on preparing to fulfill ancient prophesies by living according to pre-Columbian customs with emphasis on harmonious relationships. Tribe members learn about and experience the sweat lodge, pipe ceremony, and vision quest.

The Bear Tribe publishes *Many Smokes* magazine and fosters manufacture of Indian ware using traditional methods and designs; it also searches out opportunities for businesses to be managed by native Americans.

Early in his life, Sun Bear had a vision which directed him to teach ancestral philosophy regarding the relationship shared by all creation. In 1979, this mission brought him before audiences in Eastern cities. His wife, Wabun (Dawn Wind), shares the podium with him to speak about holistic healing and ecology.

Comanche

Quanah Parker. 1846 to 1911.

His parents were Chief Peta Nocona and Cynthia Ann Parker, a white captive whom the Comanche called Preloch. Quanah was born in the Cedar Lake region near Seminole, Texas around 1846—probably in spring which may have been the reason for his being named Kwana (Sweet Scent or Aroma). The surname Parker was added by white Texans.

Quanah's muscular physique, erect stance, and supple,

seemingly effortless movements underscored his temperament as a self-assured man. Riding low over the mane of his pony, its saddle ornamented with bits of silver and bells, rider and animal melded in a mutually complementary cadence. In battle, Quanah wore leggings, moccasins and a breechcloth, remaining naked above the waist except for a full length eagle feather headdress, large brass ear hoops and a bearclaw necklace. The Staked Plain, comprised of most of the Texas Panhandle and much of eastern New Mexico, was the favorite hunting ground of Quanah's band, the Kwahada (Antelope Eater).

In 1875, the Kwahadi were moved to Ft. Sill, Oklahoma Territory. Quanah observed and emulated white businessmen, accumulating thereby an impressive fortune that included a major share of stock in the Quanah, Acme, and Pacific Railway. He encouraged agriculture, education, and home building on the reservation. But when the U.S. Army sought volunteers for an all-Indian cavalry unit, he advised his people not to enlist. The whites wanted the Comanche to live in peace, Quanah reasoned, and that was what he intended to do; the white man's wars were not his responsibility.

Quanah lived near Cache, Oklahoma, in a two-story, thirty-two-room house with twenty-two stars on its roof; it was locally referred to as the "White House." He was elected Deputy Sheriff of Lawton, president of the local school district, and Chief Judge of the court of Indian Offenses. During his judiciary term, he was provided with an English language tutor at government expense; his judgments were always decided according to the native American philosophy of justice that crimes are committed against individuals rather than society. He kept politically informed and lobbied in Washington, D.C., for Indian rights.

Quanah disdained Christian religions but joined the Native American Church. He dressed in the style of the dominant society but donned Indian fashions for religious ceremonies. For his burial in 1911, he was attired in the type of clothing he customarily wore as a warrior chief.

Conestoga

Anonymous chief, c. 1708. *See* Eskimo, anonymous.

Conestoga chief, 1706. *See* Eskimo, anonymous.

Plains Cree

Edward Ahenakew. 1885 to 1961.

The Reverend Ahenakew was born in the Sandy Lake area of Canada in 1885. There is no Cree word for his surname, but the family was well-known locally and historically through his brother Ahtahkakoop (Star Blanket)—Chief of the House People—and Chiefs Mistawasis, Poundmaker and Red Pheasant.

As a youth, Ahenakew had an inquiring mind and excelled all other students in every activity. He entered Prince Albert—later renamed Emmanuel College—and upon graduating, became a teacher in mission schools at Sandy Lake.

He was a devout, amiable man interested in the welfare of his people, particularly the effects that white culture and reserve confinement imposed on their morale. He enrolled in Wycliffe College in Toronto to prepare for the ministry and was ordained a deacon in 1910. Ahenakew continued his studies at the theological college in Saskatoon and graduated in 1912 as Licentiate in Theology.

After his ordination, The Reverend Ahenakew was sent to the mission at Onion Lake. While there, an epidemic of influenza ravished the reserve and in his characteristic compassion, Ahenakew resolved to study medicine. He was accepted by Edmonton's medical school at the age of thirty-five. However, illness forced him to discontinue medical studies before earning a degree.

Ahenakew never marrried, instead, he devoted himself to the arduous travel demanded by missionary work. His service to the people made a lasting impression on those who knew him; twelve years after his death in 1961, Ahenakew's book, *Voices of the Plains Cree,* was published in respectful remembrance of him.

The author interprets his feelings about the experience of native Americans with white culture through Old Keyam, a representative character. In the Cree language, Keyam means "What does it matter?" or "I do not care!" The name expresses a truth or an experience. In this instance, it denotes fatalism in a milieu of unwanted and incomprehensible change. Old Keyam actually cares very much as he reviews his life from three perspectives: that of a free man, the reserve man, and the educated man living within the white community.

Father of Thunderchild. Flourished 1800s.

Swiftfootedness was an accomplishment to be proud of, especially among people who were buffalo hunters. Competitive racing was a popular sport, and as a young man, Thunderchild's father entered a race against a Stoney. The wagering was active and Thunderchild's father was nervous. The runners were well-matched, but for a while the Stoney pulled ahead and looked as if he would win. In a burst of effort as the finish line came in sight, he became so excited with the final attempt that he hadn't realized until the race was over that he had dropped his breechcloth. But he won the race.

Chief Thunderchild was in his early seventies when he told this amusing anecdote about his father.

Old Keyam. *See* Plains Cree, Edward Ahenakew.

Thunderchild. 1849 to 1927.

Cree tribesmen called him Peyasiwawasis. He lived in Canada. During early manhood, Thunderchild had been a famous foot-racer and crossed the border to hunt buffalo in Montana.

In 1881, Chief Thunderchild occupied a reserve between the Battle and Saskatchewan rivers. But in 1909, his band was moved to the Turtle Lake Reserve.

He lived according to ancient customs, but when government authorities closed the only school on his reserve, Thunderchild asked The Reverend Ahenakew to intercede to request its reopening. His appeal succeeded and the school was reopened in 1924.

Thunderchild was revered as an advisor and repository of Plains Cree lore. In order to preserve this information, he agreed a few years before his death in 1927, to have his oral renditions expressed in writing by The Reverend Edward Ahenakew. On days when he was scheduled to relate stories, an assembly of interested listeners filled the room, anxious to hear his vivid accounts of tribe members long departed but still remembered.

He was recipient of the Queen Victoria medal, and the

reserve on which he lived in a log cabin was named Thunderchild Reserve in his honor.

Creek

Hopethleycholo. 1798 to 1862.

In 1798, when Hopethleycholo was born, the Creek nation
had a long history of occupation in parts of present-day Alabama
and Georgia. They were still in possession of the land when
Andrew Jackson launched his crusade of annihilation; the battle
at Talladega, Alabama, in 1813, destroyed Creek domination of
the area.

In 1825, Hopethleycholo headed a delegation to Washington,
D.C., to persuade President John Quincy Adams to abrogate a
fraudulent treaty. It alleged that the entire Creek nation agreed to
cede all of its property in Georgia and to move west of the
Mississippi. In actuality, the signatory chiefs represented a very
small faction of the tribe. The underlying subterfuge of the land
grab was well-known within the Federal Government, nevertheless, the Senate ratified the treaty and Adams quickly penned his
signature to it.

On Adams' insistance, Secretary of War James Barbour
pressed ceaselessly for peaceful cession until the tension became
unbearable for the Creek delegates. As a compromise, Chief
Hopethleycholo and his eleven companions were willing to cede
two-thirds of the disputed land, but this did not satisfy Barbour.
Many more months passed in tedious negotiations before Barbour
succeeded in forcing the Creeks to capitulate on the government's terms: total relinquishment of the Georgia lands.

Aggrieved by the unmet needs of his people, tormented by
the implacable and relentless demands of Federal authorities, the
distraught chief attempted suicide. When news of this reached
Adams, he relented and instructed Barbour to accept the formerly
advanced compromise.

Hopethleycholo died in Kansas near Leroy Creek in 1862.

Alexander McGillivray. 1759 to 1793.

His Creek name was Hoboi Hili Miko (Good Child King).
McGillivray was born in 1759 at Little Tallassie, Alabama, to
beautiful Sehoy Marchand and wealthy fur trader Lachlan

McGillivray. He lived in a luxurious mansion with all the amenities the family's wealth easily provided. His precocity was enhanced by a classic education in schools in Charleston, South Carolina, where he acquired an interest in literary works on history which he read avidly throughout his life. He conversed mostly in French and English, and was better educated than most of the settlers who tried to dispossess the Creek Nation of its land.

By establishing trading posts in Florida and along the Gulf Coast, he became one of the wealthiest men in the South. His plantation, Apple Orchard, at Little Tallassie was his principal residence. Upon the death of his French-Creek mother, a member of the Wind Clan, he succeeded her as sachem of the Creek Nation. McGillivray was a skillful, brilliant negotiator and the nation prospered under his leadership.

To further the tribe's interests, and his own, he became Superintendent-General to the Creek Nation as representative for Spain which supplied arms for Creek warriors. During the Revolutionary War, he served as a colonel in the British forces. Later, in return for his promise to stop warring against Euro-Americans, he was paid one hundred thousand dollars and made Brigadier General in the U.S. Army. White men proved time and again that promises were made to be broken; McGillvray's promise did not preclude a primary interest in his tribe's welfare.

In 1790, McGillivray was one of twenty-nine Creek chiefs to convene in council with President George Washington in New York City. During this visit, they toured the ship *America*, which had recently returned from a voyage to Canton, China.

Although he had the full cooperation of other chiefs, the burden of managing tribal affairs was primarily McGillivray's. His efforts on behalf of the tribe gained impetus from a mix of love for his people and a lifelong hatred of Euro-Americans.

McGillivray died at Pensacola in Spanish Florida, where he was buried with Masonic honors. After his death in 1793, the large tracts of land on the Savannah and in other parts of Georgia which he had inherited from his father were confiscated by the State of Georgia.

McGillivray's half-sister, Tait, married Charles Weatherford who became the parents of William Weatherford (Red Eagle), a prominent Creek leader.

Pleasant Porter. 1840 to 1907.

To tribesmen, he was known as Talof Harjo (Crazy Bear), but in the white community he was called Pleasant Porter. He was born at Clarksville, Alabama in 1840 to Benjamin E. Porter and Phoebe, daughter of Tulope Tustunugee. Porter attended school for a short time, but was basically self-educated through extensive reading. Although he lacked formal schooling, Porter devised an effective educational system for the Creek Nation and administered it as superintendent.

His proposals for peaceful and imaginative solutions to problems arising between the Creeks and whites advanced his political career and he became a trusted emissary to promote tribal interests in Washington, D.C.

Porter was injured during the Civil War and walked with a slight but permanent limp. Standing six feet tall, black haired and bearded, he was an imposing figure at the time of his promotion to general of a Creek force in 1871. It was his duty to maintain peace among diverse factions which developed within the nation in Indian Territory. The conservative element, consisting of full-blood Creeks, advocated retention of traditional customs. Descendants of Black and Indian marriages were comprised of a large population and generally sided with the conservative view. The progressives agreed with Porter and favored adoption of white culture.

Porter, who married Mary Ellen Keys, a Cherokee, was a member of the Nation's legislative council for almost twenty years. In 1880, he was principal chief of the Muskhogee, the independent Creek Nation's last chief in Indian Territory. The Creek Nation had applied for admission to the Union as a separate state—they planned to name it Sequoyah—but their request was denied.

Porter died of a stroke in 1907 aboard a train enroute to Missouri; he was buried at Wealaka, Oklahoma.

William Weatherford. 1780 to 1826.

William Weatherford was an inventive genius who could execute his bold designs with success. Lumhe Chati (Red Eagle), as he was sometimes called, was born around 1780 in Creek Territory, Alabama, to Scotsman Charles Weatherford and Tait, the half-sister of Alexander McGillivray.

In manhood, Weatherford was handsome, tall, and physically well-endowed; his lively black eyes and thin, elegant nose gave him an aristocratically dignified appearance. A quick, yet disciplined, intellect fostered confidence in those who knew him. He was naturally reserved and spoke rarely, but when he did express himself, his arguments and dynamic eloquence persuaded others to his point of view. Before he committed himself to a major role in Creek affairs, his life was that of a comfortably well-off country gentleman. The house he built and furnished from his merchant father's stock of household goods was a source of pride and pleasure.

When Weatherford heard Tecumseh speak at the Hickory Ground village of the Creek Nation, he was inspired by the Shawnee leader's sincerity and sympathized with his views, but he was not yet active as a chief or leader in the tribe. In an 1811 speech at Tuckabatchee, present-day Alexander City, Alabama, Tecumseh made another attempt to persuade the Creeks to unite under his leadership. Once again, Weatherford was captivated by the magnetism of Tecumseh's oratory and his reasonable statements. At this time, Weatherford made his fateful decision to participate in Creek politics.

Weatherford rose rapidly to a position of authority, and established the town of Eccanachaca (Holy Ground) on the Alabama River. Another of the town's founders was the prophet Hillis Hadjo, also called Francis. In 1813, the village, with its immense properties of over two hundred houses, bountiful crops and a wealth of provisions, was destroyed by United States Army troops.

Weatherford was an impressive chief but he could not control events which enmeshed the country in the War of 1812. Friendships and animosities flowered and withered among whites and Indians alike. Weatherford attacked Ft. Mims, Alabama, in 1813. In retaliation, he was pursued without mercy. His stronghold at Horseshoe Bend was attacked in 1814 by General Andrew Jackson whom the Indians called "Sharp Knife." Heavy losses in the Creek ranks forced them to discontinue resistance to white domination. The Creek Nation and the Federal Government signed a peace treaty in 1814 at Ft. Toulouse in Wetumpka, Alabama.

Weatherford reestablished himself as a plantation owner, still an influential force in Creek–white relations as an advocate of peace. Details of this period in his life are controversial. Some reports state that he died in 1822 at his home in Polk County, Tennessee; others say he died in 1826 in Monroe County, Alabama.

Crow

Hawk. *See* Cheyenne, Hyemeyohsts Storm.

Legendary Dwarf Chief. Ancient.
Dwarf Chief is said to be a leader of the Little-People, beings who possess great physical strength and live in Medicine Rock, near Pryor, Montana. Crow legends credit them with making the stone arrow-points which are so prevalent throughout North America.

One common view supposes that small-statured races in Africa, Asia, and Oceania originated stories about dwarfs, brownies, fairies, and elves. The dwarfs of Crow and Aztec legends, the fairies in tales told in the British Isles, and the jinni of Arabian folklore are similarly endowed with magic powers; elves are usually depicted as mischievous and sometimes vengeful. There is a generally held belief in Little-People among the populace of the French province of Brittany and in Ireland.

During the 16th and 17th centuries, supposed transactions between humans and the Little-People were so widespread that the Church of Scotland undertook a vigorous campaign against them.

Mementos of the Little-People persist into the modern era. It is said that in a sunlit valley of the Blue Ridge Mountains in Virginia, fairies were dancing around a spring of still, clear water when a messenger elf arrived. Mournfully, he told them of the death of Jesus. The fairies cried on hearing the sad news; and as each tear fell to the earth, it hardened into a beautifully formed cross. They are still found by the thousands upon the ground. The fairy stone crosses, omens of good fortune, were allegedly worn by Thomas Edison, Charles Lindberg, and European royalty.

Plenty Coups. 1848 to 1932.

Native Americans call the place of his birth "The cliff that has no pass"; it is in the Crazy Mountains near Billings, Montana. His mother, Otter Woman, belonged to the Crow tribe; Medicine Bird, his father, was part Shoshone. Two of Plenty Coups' boyhood names were Swift Arrow and Faces The Buffalo North.

Having established his reputation for leadership at an early age, Plenty Coups was elected chief of a Mountain Crow band when he was twenty-five years old. Great prestige accrued to a warrior by counting coup, audaciously touching the enemy, rather than by killing him. The act permitted him to wear an eagle feather in his hair or headdress and marked him as a fearless man. Plenty Coups was renowned for the extraordinary number of times he had counted coup, earning for him the name Aleek-chea-ahoosh (Many Achievements). His war bonnet was of such length that it dragged along the ground.

The physical stamina that sustained him on the battlefield gave way to spiritual strength when dealing with white settlers. The coming of the white man was predicted in Crow legends telling of a clan leader who, because of his color, was named Mishong (Black Man). He and his people lived on Bald Mesa and were the guardians of the place where the god Bahana (White Man) was expected to arrive. Accordingly, the white man came like an avalanche, smothering the land and its people with his scorn. Plenty Coups sought inspiration for an understanding of the chaos that followed in the white man's wake by entering the Little Rocky Mountains on lonely vision quests.

As the buffalo herds decreased, Plenty Coups urged adjustment to white rule. As an example, he enlisted as an army scout and gained additional distinction for his bravery and counsel during military campaigns. He was one of the first in his tribe to become a farmer and rancher; the enterprise succeeded and he became quite wealthy.

Plenty Coups negotiated a settlement with the Northern Pacific Railroad for Crow-owned land and pressed the tribe's claim for land payments with Federal authorities. Plenty Coups was elected principal chief of the Mountain Crow in 1904.

In 1921, he represented all native Americans when he placed a wreath on the tomb of the Unknown Soldier in Arlington, Virginia.

Plenty Coups and his wife donated their home and its surrounding acreage at Pryor, Montana, to the United States. It is now a museum featuring memorabilia of Plenty Coups and the Crow tribe. Wyoming named one of its peaks near Yellowstone National Park for him, but the highest tribute came from his own people. After his death in 1932, the Crow decided that no one could equal the standard set by Plenty Coups, therefore, no one replaced him as principal chief.

Shining Arrows. *See* Cheyenne, Hyemeyohsts Storm.

Two Leggings. 1843 to 1923.

Two Leggings, a member of the Not Mixed Clan, had other names: Big Crane, and His Eyes Are Dreamy. He was born around 1843 in the Big Horn River region of Montana. His parents were Strikes At Different Camps and her husband, Four (also called No Wife).

The courage and determination that characterized his lifelong quest for religious illumination were also evident in other endeavors. Two Leggings and Plenty Coups belonged to rival warrior societies, but both had equal influence in the tribe.

Two Leggings married Ties Up Her Bundle, and until his death in 1923, they lived alongside the Big Horn near Hardin, Montana. They had a house made of timbers taken from old Ft. Custer, and a tipi which he preferred. His autobiography recounts events only to the year 1888, because after that, he said, "There is nothing more to tell."

When the town of Hardin planned its first rodeo, invitations were sent to all the chiefs. Thrilled with excitement and expectation, and dressed in his finest clothes, Two Leggings arrived in splendor at the rodeo grounds entrance. But the gatekeeper refused to admit him, for he had failed to bring his invitation. His pleas and arguments did not prevail. Two Leggings, weeping in frustration, stood outside the arena and pronounced an impassioned curse. Knowledgeable people say the Hardin rodeo has been plagued with rainy weather every since.

Voice in a vision quest.

One of the most notable characteristics of native American religious philosophy is the vision quest. This is an act of sacrifice, willingly undertaken in the hope that it will be the source of new wisdom beneficial to the people. It is also a dramatic way for the individual to test his ability to withstand the ordeals that beset his journey across the four hills: Infancy, Youth, Maturity, and Old Age.

The difference between a vision quest and Christian prayers to guardian angels and saints lies in the personal commitment required of the native American. Fasting in solitude, a seeker would persevere for a long time, and often refused to terminate his quest except at the urgings of a medicine man or family and friends. It was not necessarily a single experience; a vision quest could be attempted as often as the individual felt a need to commune with the All-Pervading Power.

According to Black Elk, the Crying for a Vision ritual predates the use of the Sacred Pipe and is the source of the four great rites of the Sioux. Crying for a Vision, or Lamenting, is chosen for many reasons, but most important is its metaphysical effect. The successful dreamer attains a realization of Oneness with all creation and an understanding of Wakonda, the source of all creation. Revelations received during the vision quest dream are assurances or affirmations that the All Pervading Power blesses the seeker, who then responds by a show of utmost confidence in the protection of his spirit guide.

The mystic experience can be preserved in song, and important elements painted on tipi or shield, but the full content of the dream is never revealed except to holy men or medicine men knowledgeable in symbolism, and who are the definitive interpreters of visions.

White Wolf. *See* Cheyenne, Hyemeyohsts Storm.

Delaware

Hopocan. 1725 to 1794.

Chief Hopocan (Tobacco Pipe), born around 1725, was a hereditary sachem of the Wolf Clan. Colonists referred to him as Captain Pipe. The tribe's villages once lined the Delaware River, but after 1720 they occupied the Muskingum Valley in Ohio.

Situated between the British colonists and the military forces in Canada who were loyal to the king of England, Hopocan became involved in their disputes. He had always disliked the land-hungry colonists and chose to side with the royalists whose main interest was the preservation of the mercantile system for the mother country. Hopocan was a perceptive, gifted orator and spoke at many conferences held at Ft. Pitt and Ft. Harmar.

In 1763, he began using the name Konieschguanokee (Maker Of Daylight), and made an unsuccessful attack on Ft. Pitt, Pennsylvania. As conflicts intensified in 1780, Hopocan moved his band to a place near White Woman's Town, Ohio. During the War of Independence, Hopocan allied with Chief Wingenim and the English to defeat a colonial militia near Upper Sandusky, Ohio.

At the time of his death in 1794, Hopocan was living in a village named for him on the Sandusky River in Ohio.

Tadeuskund. 1700 to 1763.

His name means "The Healer" or possibly "Earth Trembler"; he belonged to the Turtle Clan of the Delaware tribe. Tadeuskund was born around 1700 in the area comprising Trenton, New Jersey. But when he was about thirty years old, he established a village beside the Delaware in Pennsylvania. During the twenty-five years that followed, the tribe lost much of its land to white encroachment and fraudulent sales; tribe leaders protested, but without resorting to arms. The people became impoverished, supporting themselves by selling brooms and baskets to white settlers. Tadeuskund gained a reputation for fair dealing in his transactions and the whites nicknamed him "Honest John."

With his wife, Elizabeth, he moved to the Christian Indian settlement established by the Moravian Church along the Mahoning River. At the time of his baptism in 1750, he was named Gideon. Tadeuskund remained with the missionaries until the threat of English and French expansion in the area, and Iroquoian disdain for the Delaware's meek acceptance of it, became intolerable.

He became a chief in 1754, and severed the tribe's ties to the Iroquois. Tadeuskund then negotiated with the Europeans on terms relevant to his own people's interests. Constantly alert to opportunities that benefitted the Delaware, he took advantage of such occasions to obtain concessions or a fair exchange of goods.

In 1756, Tadeuskund attended a general congress of English and native Americans in Easton, Pennsylvania. It was convened to promote friendly relations between the two races. His cooperation ensured success to British forces in the battle at Ft. Duquesne in 1758. In that year, the chief's village was near Bethlehem, Pennsylvania.

He spared no effort to live in harmony with the Europeans, but negotiated skillfully to insure such tranquility at the least cost to the Delaware and their allies, the Shawnee and Mahican tribes. However, he became increasingly disenchanted with the whites because of their deceitfulness.

Tadeuskund burned to death in a fire that engulfed his house at Wajomick in 1763.

Wingenim. Flourished 1700s.

His name—variously spelled Wingenimi, Wingina, and Wingenund—means "He Approves" or "He Is Pleased With." It may have been of honorary or hereditary derivation, for it appears frequently in journals of colonial Roanoke Island, Virginia—present-day North Carolina.

Events in his early life are unknown, but in later years, he was active in opposing white expansion into tribal lands. Wingenim led the Delaware into battle against the colonists in the War of Independence. However, he did develop a friendship with Colonel William Crawford who was defeated and captured by Hopocan at Upper Sandusky, Ohio, in 1782. Crawford was sentenced to die in retaliation for previously committed atrocities by some of the men in his unit against the Christian Indians. Wingenim was asked to intercede on Crawford's behalf. But Chief Wingenim was a strict observer of the native American code of honor and justice which called for restitution to an injured party. He explained that the tradition was so deeply rooted that nothing could alter it, not even if the king of England appeared with all of his treasures and wealth. It was a tribal law, and he alone could not control or deviate from the will of the people—not even to save his own best friend.

Duwamish

Seattle. 1785 to 1866.

He was born around 1785 to Woodsholitsa of the Duwamish tribe, near Seattle, Washington. At an early age, he prepared for the day when he would succeed his father, chief Schweabe, by fasting and seeking spirit sight to provide the power and wisdom expected in a leader. During one vision, he saw the Suquamish symbol of peace, a seagull flying with its wings fully extended. While still a boy, he helped to build the one-thousand-foot-long Old Man House along the shore of Puget Sound.

Seattle was around seven years old when he witnessed the arrival of George Vancouver aboard the *Discovery* as it sailed up Puget Sound in 1792; it was his first view of a white man.

At age twenty-two, he became head chief of the Duwamish and Suquamish. It is said, that when addressing a large gathering, Seattle could easily and comfortably be heard by those a half mile away.

He married a Duwamish woman named Ladaila; after she died, he married Oihl. Seattle sired six children. In 1838, he was baptized in Roman Catholic rites and named Noah.

Seattle was mild mannered and kindly; expecting relief from white harassment, he signed the Treaty of Port Eliot in 1855. Thus, confining his people to Port Madison Reservation where he lived at the time of his death in 1866. He was buried near Old Man House in the Suquamish cemetery. A statue of the chief stands in Seattle at Fifth and Denny streets.

Eskimo

Anonymous.

Anonymity has often been a result of the native American belief that it is dangerous to mention names of the dead because it angers and activates the soul of the departed. Reluctance to provide names has also frequently been due to a desire to avoid desecration of graves by whites in search of valuables interred with the deceased. In other instances, identification is unavailable because early historians failed to record the information.

Additionally, the characteristic modesty of native Americans encourages anonymity. Habitually accustomed to making accurate statements of fact, they do not credit themselves as the originators of traditional information and often preface their statements with "It is said," signifying thereby, that the data conveyed was obtained from another source, such as the Ancient Ones. In this way, native Americans refer to the beginning or original source and credit their culture rather than themselves.

Fox

Black Thunder. Flourished mid-1700s to early 1800s.

Makatananamaki (Black Thunder) was considered a patriarch when he attended the treaty councils at Portage, Wisconsin in 1815. He was an honorable man of high principles; he kept his word and expected others to do likewise. An air of quiet thoughtfulness about him inspired respect, and his opinions were highly esteemed. However, Black Thunder bristled with indignation when anyone belittled the moral code of native Americans; he knew that white accusers were guilty themselves of the faults they tried to place upon his people.

Typically, Black Thunder was an excellent speaker. So finely honed were the skills of oratory and debate among native Americans, that the U.S. Government assigned its most capable men to negotiate treaties.

Singing Around Rite. Ancient.

Those who belong to the Fox Society are known as "They who go about singing"; the *Singing Around* rite explains and describes the ancient origin of the society. Membership is by invitation, and when a member dies, a new one is elected to fill his place during the adoption-feast. Ceremonial observances of the rite serve as reminders and examples of the high moral standards expected of the people. They include a retelling of the story of Has An Eye And Is Sitting, who from the age of five began to sit for lessons from his grandfather. The exemplary conduct taught to this youth formed the basis of the Fox tribe's moral philosophy. The *Singing Around* rite relates that by observing these rules of conduct, and by fasting and vigil, one will receive blessings enabling him to obtain game easily, to be a leader in any endeavor, and to help the people in their daily living.

Tribe mother. *See* Oglala Sioux, village elder.

White Buffalo. Ancient.

Lore regarding White Buffalo is so ancient that it has become shrouded in myth and mystery. White Buffalo is the physical materialization of a guardian spirit that permeates the moral and metaphysical consciousness of native Americans. Otherwise, it is invisible and moves in a dimension attuned to the realm of supernatural spirits. It cares for the life of the people and they in turn honor it in ceremony, song, and dance.

White Buffalo Dance. Ancient.

This is a very sacred ceremony performed so the earth may be beautiful, to bring good health, and to assure benefits after death by worshiping during life. Participants are required to fast, as this increases the possibility of aid from supernatural powers. The White Buffalo Dance incorporates the experiences of ancestors who were the first to be taught the rite, and their instructions for its reenactment.

Legend states that White Buffalo had red eyes and red horns to confirm that the people's blessings came from an uncommon source.

The ceremony requires specifically prescribed items, such as a white buffalo hide, sacred packs, tobacco, young pups, fire, drum, flute, gourds, sugar, and a catlinite pipe with feather-decorated stem. It is an elaborate undertaking necessitating the cooperation of many people in a way that provides an opportunity for them to practice the rules of behavior embodied in White Buffalo's instructions. There is music, feasting and dancing, each a meaningful reminder of customs handed down by White Buffalo and observed by every generation from antiquity to modern times.

Hidatsa

Edward Goodbird. 1869 to ?

At the time of his birth in 1869, his maternal grandfather, Small Ankle, named him Tsakakasaki (Good Bird). His parents, Son Of A Star and Mahidiwia (Buffalo Bird Woman), sent him to mission schools where he learned to speak English at age seven.

The first December of his first school year was also the first time he saw a Christmas tree and learned the meaning of the Christian holiday. He found much to excite him, but his greatest pleasure came from singing the songs he was taught.

Goodbird was twelve years old when he accompanied his father on a buffalo hunt dressed in moccasins, leggings and a vest of black cloth embroidered with elk teeth that his mother made. While still in his youth, he joined the Grass Dance and was made an officer. This called for special recognition. To honor the occasion, Son Of A Star hung a splendid eagle feather headdress in the family lodge.

Goodbird became an interpreter on the Ft. Berthold Reservation in North Dakota. He also farmed and was so successful in adopting methods taught by his instructor, that he was appointed assistant to the agency farmer. In 1904, he was an assistant missionary at Independence Hill, and each Sunday he interpreted the *Bible* in Hidatsa, the language of his congregation.

He liked to hunt and was fond of recalling a strange incident: after taking aim and killing a buck, he proceeded to where the animal had been dropped; to his amazement, he found that he had also shot with the single bullet a doe which stood behind the buck, hidden from Goodbird's view when he took aim.

Goodbird still lived on the Ft. Berthold Reservation in 1913 when he dictated for publication a brief history of the Hidatsa tribe.

Hopi

A mother's counsel. *See* Oglala Sioux, village elder.

Ethic. *See* Cherokee, ethic.

Old Ones. Ancient.

The word "old" is a term of respect which acknowledges that those so addressed gained their wisdom from long years of experience and contemplation. According to one account in the Sacred Legend, seven old men gathered to ponder ways of holding the people together. After lengthy deliberation, they inaugurated a central governing council to provide the common unifying bond they were seeking. Their decision was based on earlier forms that took into consideration the realities of existing conditions and the ancient beliefs and ideas of the people in regard to humankind's relation to the cosmos. The result was the formation of a representative form of government.

Oral tradition. *See* Cherokee, ethic.

Proverb. *See* Apache, proverb.

Polingaysi Qoyawayma. 1892 to ____.

In the Hopi language, Polingaysi means "Butterfly Sitting Among The Flowers In The Breeze." A member of the Coyote Clan, she was born in 1892 and lived with her parents, Sevenka and Fred Qoyawayma, in New Oraibi, Arizona. Elizabeth Ruth White, the name she adopted in later years, had an insatiable curiosity for the new, the different. Her eyes were always directed to the distant horizon for fresh adventures in learning.

She attended Sherman Institute in Riverside, California, and later entered Bethel Academy. Polingaysi had a beautiful singing voice—strong, sweet, clear, true, and capable of sustaining high notes. Therefore, her studies included vocal and piano instructions. Ambitious and eager to be educated, she earned tuition by working at any jobs available. Her continual search for opportunities to challenge her many talents was sustained by a determination to succeed.

When Polingaysi began to teach, she initiated innovative and effective methods appropriate to the needs of her native American pupils. Among the educators in the Indian Service during 1941, she was chosen to demonstrate her techniques to supervisors and instructors assembled in Chemawa, Oregon. Her approach to education was practical as well as novel, and the Arizona State Teachers College invited the children's primary rhythm band she had organized to present a program of music.

Polingaysi retired from teaching in 1954, but remained active on behalf of native Americans. She has had an autobiography published, and founded an association to solicit scholarship funds for native American students.

Sevenka Qoyawayma. ? to 1951.

Like other members of the Coyote Clan who possess prophetic powers, Sevenka was a visionary who could interpret dreams. She lived on the Hopi Reservation at New Oraibi, Third Mesa, Arizona, in a stone house built by her husband.

She belonged to the Mazhrau Women's Society, a dancing and singing group. Sevenka composed songs for the society, including one that was used for many years by the Niman Dancers in the late July ceremony that closes the Kachina calendar.

Mazhrau members devote long hours to learning the society's songs and fitting them to dance steps, for the songs have not been recorded and must be memorized by each performer. Remembrance must be accurate, for these songs are living prayers. Sevenka's speaking voice was as melodious and pleasant to hear as was her singing voice.

Sevenka was the wife of Fred Qoyawayma who worked for the Mennonite missionaries, and the mother of Polingaysi (Elizabeth Ruth White).

Song of the Long Hair Kachinas. Ancient.

The legendary retreat of the Kachin, supernatural beings, are the snowcapped San Francisco Peaks of Arizona. In the beginning of time, the Kachin brought the plaque of many seeds and saved the people from starvation.

In Hopi religion, Kachinas represent the spirit essence of all that is found in the real world. They are not worshipped, but are thought of as friends and benefactors interested in Hopi welfare. More than two hundred important Kachina figures are repre-sented in Kachina dances. Kachina impersonators act as interme-diaries between the visible and spirit worlds; their masks and costumes are made by priests in the kivas. Men who represent female figures are called Kachinmanas.

Children play with flat, toy Kachina dolls that are adorned with bright paint and feathers, but the three dimensional dolls, or *Tihu*, which are distributed as gifts on the last day of each festival, are not playthings. Made of cottonwood root, *Tihu* are elaborately clothed effigies of the Kachin impersonated in the Dance. Kachina dolls are internationally prized by collectors.

Don Talayesva. 1890 to _____.

His parents were Chief Yokeoma and Hahaye. Don Talayesva grew up among the Hopi at Oraibi, Arizona. He learned to speak

English when ten years old, and at a later age, became a healer and head of the Sun Clan.

Talayesva is a shepherd in harmony with the cadence of nature's seasonal changes, searching continuously for grazing pastures in the arid plateau region of his home. Conscientiously attending to the secular and spiritual duties that vie for his time and energy, the chief is an important person in the lives of the people.

Winter months are passed in making snowshoes out of sheepskins, and participating in the December Soyal when members gather in the kiva to pray and sing for a good crop in the coming summer, and for an increase in the creatures of the earth. Deeply religious, Talayesva is an ardent advocate of traditional customs in spite of the changes intruding upon his pastoral life.

Industrial and commercial development, especially on the Navajo Reservation which surrounds the Hopi, is rapidly propelling the people into the space age. However, they intend to travel that road on their own terms.

Traditional teaching. *See* Omaha, moral teaching.

Village elders. *See* Oglala Sioux, village elder.

Iowa

Moanahonga. ? to 1834.

His several names were reminiscent of his many accomplishments. Among them: Great Walker—because he showed strength and endurance while chasing game, and could lead war parties across long stretches of territory without indication of fatigue; Winaugusconey (The Man Who Is Not Afraid To Travel)—bestowed for his ability to travel alone without fear through any country, depending solely upon his fortitude and courage to overcome adversity; and Big Neck.

His chieftainship was earned, for Moanahonga was a poor boy who rose through the ranks of braves, proving by deeds that he had the qualities of a leader. In 1824, he went to Washington, D.C., to contest ownership of land, in Missouri, which the government claimed had been ceded by a treaty with the Osage in 1808. Unsuccessful in regaining the property, he returned to Missouri and made an effort to comply with the treaty terms. However, the Iowa were frustrated by local settlers and newspaper accounts which exaggerated frontier incidents, always to the detriment of native Americans. Misunderstandings and agitation for their removal forced Moanahonga into a defensive posture against Federal troops and state militias. The Iowa chief was captured and taken to Keokuk, Iowa, as a prisoner of war and tried for murder in Randolph County, Missouri, even though his actions had been against military personnel rather than civilians. The jury, without leaving the courtroom for further consideration, delivered a "not guilty" verdict.

After his release, Moanahonga blackened his face as a sign of mourning for the loss of his ancestral land and the subjugation of his people by the dominant society. He wore black face paint until his death in 1834.

White Cloud. 1812 to ?

White Cloud was born into adversity around 1812, and remained a melancholy figure throughout his life. He was only twenty-four when he succeeded his father, Mahaskah (White Cloud), as principal chief of the Iowa. His mother, Rantchewaime (Female Flying Pigeon), was the only woman among the Iowa delegation sent to Washington, D.C., in 1824.

Twelve years later their son, White Cloud, also entrained for the nation's capital. Traveling at his own expense, he went to discuss the flagrant disregard of treaties, provocations by settlers invading tribal land, and the failure of Federal agents to protect the tribe's rights.

Several removals within a short time added to the Iowa's afflictions. The tribe's ancestral territory became the state of Iowa. They moved again after surrendering their land in northern Missouri in 1824. By 1829, the tribe encamped along the Platte River in Nebraska. In 1836, when White Cloud was chief, the people were dispersed on reservations in Kansas and Oklahoma.

Between 1844 and 1845, White Cloud was one of fourteen Iowa accompanying George Catlin's Indian Gallery Exposition in Europe. He traveled with his wife, Rutonyewema (Strutting Pigeon), and their daughter, Wisdom. Jeffrey Doraway, born of Black and Caucasian parents but reared among the Iowa, was their interpreter. He was introduced to audiences as an Indian.

According to Catlin, White Cloud was about five feet ten inches tall; his features could be described as "Roman" with a benign expression; and he seemed self-conscious about a defect in one eye.

Death and sickness plagued the troupe, bringing the tour to an early end. White Cloud returned to the sixteen acres of land he cultivated on the Upper Missouri near the Rocky Mountains. He did his own plowing, and after harvesting the crops, retained only enough for his family's needs, donating the remainder to the poor among his people.

Iroquois

Chief's address in council. *See* Eskimo, anonymous.

Kanickhungo. Flourished 1700s.

His tribe belonged to the mighty Five Nations Iroquois Confederacy that helped to shape American history when it chose to assist the British in establishing forts and settlements, thereby, limiting French power and influence. The chiefs and sachems governed the tribes of the Ohio Valley from their meeting place at present-day New Castle, Pennsylvania.

Chief Kanickhungo flourished during the 1700s when colonists still pledged their loyalty to foreign sovereigns and only native Americans had an affinity for the North American continent. Ambitious adventurers and seekers of religious freedom—Swedes, Finns, Germans, Scots-Irish and English—arrived by boat in Philadelphia's port. Its strategic location and burgeoning economy made it the center of colonial commerce.

The town of Azilum near Towanda, Pennyslvania, was established as a refuge for French nobility fleeing the revolution. The largest of this town's buildings was called La Grande Maison; it was built for Queen Marie Antoinette had she succeeded in escaping. The town of Loretto, Pennyslvania, was founded by Prince Gallitzin as a Catholic colony; the prince–priest was later disinherited by the Russian emperor because of his religion. Philadelphia was a melange of pioneers, and it was to them, that Kanickhungo addressed his speech in a council of native Americans and whites in 1736.

Kiowa

N. Scott Momaday. 1934 to ____.

Navarre Scott Momaday, born in 1934 at Lawton, Oklahoma, is the son of author Natachee Scott and popular painter Al Momaday. After completing the twelfth grade at Virginia Military Academy, Momaday entered the University of New Mexico. Upon graduation, he became a teacher on the Jicarilla Apache Reservation at Dulce, New Mexico. Later, Momaday earned M.A. and Ph.D. degrees from Stanford University, and in 1962 joined the faculty at the University of California, Santa Barbara. In 1966, he became Associate Professor of English and Comparative Literature at Berkeley where he inaugurated a course in American Indian literature; since then, he has held this position at Stanford University.

He is a recipient of the John Hay Whitney Fellowship, the Woodrow Wilson Award, Stanford Creative Writing Fellowship in Poetry (1959-1960), Guggenheim Fellowship (1966-1967), and the Pulitzer Prize for fiction (1969).

If Momaday counted coups, as his ancestors did, on white culture, his eagle feather headdress would be magnificently splendid in recording his achievements. Professor Momaday renews his link with the past each July Fourth when he begins a pilgrimage from his home in California to Carnegie, Oklahoma, where he meets with other Taimpe Society members to perform the Gourd Dance. His young daughters Cael, Jill and Brit, accompany him to observe the ancient rite. Wearing moccasins, white trousers with beaded tassels at his right leg and a black velvet waist sash, he dons a bandoleer of red beans and a blanket before joining the dancers. The bandoleer belonged to his grandfather, Mammedaty (Sky Walker).

Satanta. 1830 to 1878.

Around the time of his birth in 1830, the Kiowa occupied the Arkansas River region; he was then called Gúaton Bain (Big Ribs). Following a land cession treaty in 1837, the tribe moved to the Texas Panhandle where he grew to manhood.

Satanta (White Bear) was one of the most extraordinary characters to appear on the Western frontier. Alone or in a group, he commanded attention. He was over six feet tall, broad shouldered and thick chested; his muscular arms and legs obviated strength and vigor. Although he was gigantic in size, his gait was graceful. Satanta had jet-black hair worn in a single braided scalplock adorned with a solitary eagle feather. Seated on his horse, he evoked a vision of chiseled mohogany. Satanta's diplomacy, imaginative politicizing and delightful humor won for him a chieftainship before his thirty-seventh birthday. After 1867, the Kiowa were moved to Indian Territory, but Satanta continued to raid into Texas. In battle, Satanta carried an army bugle to direct his warriors; these signals became his trademark. To announce mealtime at home, he blew vigorously on a brass French horn.

His love affairs were legion and legendary. Satanta spoke fluent Kiowa, Comanche and Spanish, and could make himself understood in Pueblo and English.

Satanta never overlooked an opportunity to address an assemblage, whether large or small. He found inordinate pleasure in public speaking, and was particularly gratified by his ability to engross his listeners. Journalists of 1867 called him the "Orator of the Plains." He enjoyed pomp and did everything with a touch of noble glory. When Satanta attended a peace or war council, he arrived triumphantly, his body painted brilliant red. To mark the occasion, his tipi was also painted bright red and topped with long red streamers attached to poles high above the ground.

During his imprisonment in 1871 to await trial for the deaths of several white men who were killed in an attack, Satanta remained lean and agile; his princely carriage made even prison garb appear elegant. He was assigned to manufacture chairs, but refused to comply with the order. Instead, he agreed to make small souvenirs such as bows and arrows to sell to the public, doing so more to escape boredom than to oblige prison authorities. The Kiowa chief was sentenced for life, but won parole after two years. He was rearrested in 1874 on allegedly unfounded charges.

His bleak future oppressed him, and in 1878, he slashed his neck and leg arteries. Guards moved him to a room for medical treatment, but he plunged from the second floor window and died. In 1963, his body was exhumed from Felson's Field outside the walls of the Huntsville, Texas penitentiary, at the request of his grandson, James Auchiah of Carnegie, Oklahoma. Chief Satanta was accorded full military honors and reburied in the Ft. Sill post cemetery at Lawton, Oklahoma.

Kwakiutl

Charles James Nowell. 1870 to ?

The Kwakiutl live on Vancouver Island, British Columbia; Nowell was born there in 1870 at Fort Rupert. He was orphaned at an early age; therefore, his training and guidance came from his older brother. During early childhood, Nowell was called Tlalis (Stranded Whale). At the age of twelve, he was given a new name: Tlakodlas (Where You Get Your Coppers From). While attending school, he was baptized and named Charles James Nowell in honor of his godfather, a school teacher in England who provided material and monetary support. At twenty, he was named Husemdas to signify that he, by his brother's consent, was to take the brother's position in the clan and inherit his estate upon the kin's death.

Nowell performed in a dance exhibition at the St. Louis Exposition in Missouri. Afterwards, he went to Chicago to set up an authentic model of the Kwakiutl in a typical setting; Nowell also lectured and answered questions in English when querried by exhibit viewers. He then toured New York museums to critically appraise their Indian displays.

At home he was in charge of employing Indian fishermen for a fish cannery, in addition to giving conscientious regard to his duties as a chief.

Into maturity, Nowell was a handsome man with the glow of youthful good health that reflected his outdoor environment and belied his age. When seventy years old, he dictated an autobiography in which his candid opinions and statements of fact provide a rare, intimate glimpse of tribal mores.

Maricopa

Last Star. 1866 to ?

Since he was his parents' only child, they named him Last Star; when one sees the last star in the sky, it is the only one. Born around 1866, he lived on the Gila River Reservation in Arizona where the Maricopa have resided since 1800. In later years, he used the name Thomas Sak O Par. As was typical among the people of this tribe, Last Star was very knowledgeable in astronomy. The Maricopa believe that above the sky is a duplicate of the Earth world.

The Maricopa have adopted a modern lifestyle and modern conveniences, but their interpersonal relationships are still governed by ancient traditions and customs.

Namet. Ancient.

According to the Maricopa who live on the Gila River Reservation in Arizona, it was Namet, the older brother of Coyote, who decreed that humans will be responsible for building their own houses, shall sing for the sick and the dead, be forgiving, and that men shall fight over women. At that time, when all things were being created for Earth, Namet also decided that the rain clouds to make plants grow shall come from the South.

Animals frequently figure in the creation stories of North American Indian tribes. Coyote's role varies according to the lesson being taught, he is most often featured as a foolish animal who creates difficult situations for himself as a result of gluttony, avarice, pride, or disobedience. His adventures are portrayed to teach right conduct.

In an allegorical explanation of why people get sick and die, Coyote—who knows everything—and Namet are symbolic characters illustrating moral principles and abstract truths. By this means, the people are given an understanding of the reason for continuing ancient beliefs and customs.

Meskwaki

Harry Lincoln. Flourished early 1900s.

In conjunction with ethnologists and anthropologists, Lincoln contributed to the preservation of customs, traditions and interpretations of sacred songs and ceremonies which might otherwise have been lost.

Lincoln's works include a translation of *The Way Meskwakies Do When They Die*; he assisted with the phonetics for the text of *Notes on the Fox Society, Known As Those Who Worship the Little*

Spotted Buffalo, and helped analyze the written texts of Alfred Kiyana whose brother, Kapayou, was guardian of the ceremonials which were the basic sources for the work *White Buffalo Dance of the Fox Indians.*

He was also instrumental in obtaining data for *Fox Mortuary Customs and Beliefs,* providing information on ethnological as well as linguistic matters pertaining to Fox culture, and arranging the recording of the origin of the *Singing Around Rite.* His wife, Dalottiwa, worked as project assistant to resolve phonetic problems encountered in transcribing the history of the Fox tribe.

Harry Lincoln followed ancient customs, and was a ceremonial attendant at the White Buffalo Dance held on June 13, 1924.

Manito. Ancient.

Manito is a term applied to a spirit with supernatural powers, or an object that is endowed with the spirit's qualities, and connotes sacredness or holiness worthy of respect and reverence. Manitos are greater than man, but lesser than the Uncreated Creator, who act as intermediaries between man and the All-permeating Life Force. They are analogous to Christian angels who are messengers of God known by individual names in some instances.

Also similar to Christian religion, the spirits can be good or evil. Osage genesis legends tell of the mythical man with cloven feet named Little Earth whom the people set out to destroy; Iya is an evil spirit in Lakota cosmology. The hermaphrodite Natliyil-hatse is the spirit leader of the lower world to which she descended after her death according to Navajo accounts. Wind spirits Gaoh (Iroquois), Hotoru (Pawnee) and Takuskanskan (Sioux) are benevolent manitos.

Manabozho, the manito of the East, was chosen by the Spirits of the Four Directions to descend to Earth and become Man. The Ojibwa say he was born on Madeline Island in Lake Superior to a virgin mother and became mankind's first teacher and the source of all gifts but Immortality.

Greater than all manitos is he who has his origin from no one but himself, the Uncreated Creator. Although his name varies according to tribe and time, the central belief in the existence of a universal spirit remains unchanged.

Modoc

Kintpuash. 1834 to 1873.

Kintpuash (He Has Water Brash) was born around 1834 in the Lost River village of Wachamshwash, the son of a chief. White settlers derisively called him Captain Jack because he wore military-style clothing of his own design. He was descended from prominent men whose ancestral home was the Tule Lake–Lost River region of California.

In 1864, the Modoc were moved to an Oregon reservation already occupied by the Klamath tribe. When the land area proved inadequate to support both tribes, Kintpuash led a group of Modoc to California where they asked government authorities for a parcel of ancestral land; the request was denied. White settlers considered the Modoc intruders and demanded their removal. A military unit was sent to the Modoc camp to force their return to Oregon; both sides sustained casualties during the encounter. In the aftermath, the Modoc fled to the barren Lava Beds in Northern California where they kept the United States Army at bay for six months.

Death stalked Time and the Modoc leaders followed in its trail. The peace parley that had been arranged ended quickly when the principal negotiating officer, General Edward R. Canby, was killed during a scuffle. The Modoc were arrested en masse and brought before a military court, to be judged by the same men they fought against.

Kintpuash and three of his band were sentenced to die by hanging; the rest of his followers were removed to Oklahoma. After the sentence was carried out at Ft. Klamath on October 3, 1873, the body of Kintpuash was taken to Yreka, California, and put on display. For an admission fee of ten cents, the curious public could view the mighty Modoc's corpse. A movie based on this incident in his life was released in 1954.

Peter Sconchin. 1850 to ?

At the time of his birth around 1850 near Tule Lake, California, the Modoc occupied territory in the boldly sculptured region along the California and Oregon border. He was a nephew of powerful Modoc leader Chief Sconchin (He Who Goes With His Head Thrust Outward), and the son of John Sconchin, second in command to Kintpuash with whom he was sentenced to die in 1873.

In the history of this tribe's several removals, Peter Sconchin lived on the Klamath Reservation in Oregon, and the Quapaw Reservation in Oklahoma. In 1887, he returned to live among the Klamath, the tribe of his wife Lizzie.

Peter Sconchin learned to speak English to facilitate his dealings with government agents, but never fully participated in white culture.

He had always been a devout man; however, in his declining years, Sconchin's concept of religion changed. He rejected Christian theology and many traditional native American beliefs. The religious synthesis that evolved from this reflected his reverence for the Creative Force in whom he felt the utmost confidence: the Sun.

Mohican

Apaumet. Flourished mid-1800s.

Classmates and professors at Princeton University, New Jersey, knew him as John Calvin. He was schooled in classical courses of the gentleman scholar, and in English literature. Apaumet used his remarkably retentive memory to amaze and entertain friends by reciting long passages from the writings of Homer, a favorite pastime among *literati* of the 1800s.

After completing his studies at Princeton, Apaumet returned to his village on the Housatonic River and later accompanied the tribe when it moved to the Oneida in western New York. He soon realized that he was untrained as a hunter, fisherman, or in any of the other skills that would have eased his assimilation into the Mohican's mode of living. He became a schoolmaster, but the yoke of conformity and servitude that typified Victorian white culture conflicted with the freedom and individuality that marked his own.

Trained for the white man's world which he disliked, but unfit for the native American lifestyle he admired, Apaumet eventually became profoundly demoralized by this dilemma. He often remarked that his knowledge was useless to him, for the history he had been taught revealed that he and his people were savages, and he now was an "educated savage." To the end of his life, he never succeeded in reconciling his heritage with his training.

Navajo

Ancient legend. Ancient.

Poverty and its antithesis, *abundance,* are but two of many significant themes in legends that are as old as man's conscious image of himself. They are historical realities which parallel a people's experience of the physical and spiritual life and reveal the centuries-long maturity of native American philosophy. From their perception of the conceptual and actual condition have evolved such powerful legends as the Corn Spirit in the Algonquian story of Mondawmin, the Navajo account of Creation, the Pueblo Corn Dance, and the White Buffalo Calf Woman of the Sioux.

It Was the Wind. Pre-Columbian.

This Navajo account of the First Man and First Woman recalls the biblical Adam and Eve. Wind, along with Sun, Earth, Water and Vegetation, is considered to be one of the powers that sustains life. Of these five lesser powers, Wind was the first to intercede between the All-Permeating Life Force and man—it is the breath of life that animated man and left as a reminder on human finger tips an imprint of itself in the form of a whirlwind.

Wind, from its position in the Four Directions, guards the path down which all lesser powers must travel when they descend to Earth to help mankind. This mighty spirit who brings life can also destroy it. Therefore, native Americans glorify and honor it in song and rite, and ask protection against its destructive influence. In a ceremonial offering, the calumet is always raised to the Wind; it is the essence of life, controlling the seasons and weather. Wind is the precursor of rain which signified fertility, growth and salvation.

When characters such as Wind, Rain, and animals with human attributes appear in stories, they are not to be thought of as human. The important qualities to note are the cause and effect of actions, emotions, and attitudes.

Left Handed. 1868 to ?

Left Handed belonged to the Bitahni Clan. In the year of his birth, 1868, the Navajo Nation signed a treaty permitting them to occupy a reservation located in three states: Utah, Arizona, and New Mexico.

Not a robust child, Left Handed was encouraged to race. From the first day in December to the last day in January, with courageous determination, he would rise early each morning while it was still dark. Although snow blanketed the ground, he donned only a breechcloth and moccasins filled with sand to toughen his feet and make his leg muscles hard and strong. He ran for six miles, then plunged into a cold river for a swim. The water on his body soon turned to ice, crackling as he raced back to the hogan.

When Left Handed was fourteen, his family moved its sheep and horses to the verdant pastures at Navajo Mountain, Utah. On the way they stopped at Sweet Water, Two Red Rocks Pointing Together, Dry Around The Water, Flowering Through Rocks, and spent part of the season close to the river by a rocky hill the Navajo called Coiled Mountain. The scenic grandeur and sun-dominated climate lent an air of romance to the guilelessly named places in the mind of a boy on the threshhold of manhood.

Mother's traditional advice. *See* Oglala Sioux, village elder.

Old Mexican. 1866 to ?

In youth, he was called Big Mexican. Born in 1866 near Shaly Rock Point and Oraibi, Arizona, from an early age he was trained to be industrious and self-reliant. At age five, he was given a goat and expected to provide total care of the animal. The goat was intended to supply income to support all of the youngster's personal necessities.

Big Mexican was seven years old when his father died, and the boy assumed additional responsibilities. By the time he was eleven, Big Mexican shared the family work-load by shearing sheep, chopping wood, hoeing, harvesting, and watering and feeding the horses. Tenacious and enterprising, Big Mexican succeeded in becoming a "man of property" when only thirteen years old. He owned three horses and thirty-three sheep and goats—all the result of his skillful animal husbandry and shrewd business acumen. He also planted crops for his own consumption.

Most of his years as an adult were spent in Sweetwater and Aneth where he was known as a swift racer, avid deer hunter and a man of above-average intelligence. Ingenuity and originality were evident in Big Mexican's deeds and expressed thoughts; he avoided displays of aggression. Flexible and pragmatic, he blended elements of white culture into his own for a self-satisfactory synthesis. There is an admirably enduring quality of moral fortitude, courage, and determination woven through Big Mexican's life; and he nearly attained the ideal that the Navajo strive for. His good name and reputation were a source of pride, and he was careful to retain both.

At age sixty-three, he was stricken with a disabling illness and taken to Wooded Hill Point. With advancing age, he became paralyzed and bedridden; the people began referring to him as Old Mexican rather than Big Mexican. Unable to care for himself, he moved to his oldest sister's hogan where he was destined to live out his allotted Earth time.

Undaunted, Old Mexican relied on absolute will-power each day to drag himself on elbows across the floor and into the sunlight outside the hogan. There he would sit, finding enormous pleasure in the warmth of the day and the continually changing landscape. To such a man, the pain of illness was less intense than the pain of losing his independence.

Oral tradition. *See* Cherokee, ethic.

Song of the Young War God. Ancient.
Song of the Young War God is a Nightway chant. Whether viewed as prayer, allegory, legend or literature, the songs of the Kledzhe Hatal (Night Chant or Nightway) belong among the world's greatest compositions. They are rich in symbolism and beautiful imagery reflecting twinness or pairing. Nightway is a sacred ceremony relating the story of the Ni Nahoka Dine (People Of The Earth). Nightway is analytical and progressive in composition, and typifies the people's attitude toward all things—it is a *whole.* All parts are represented: the sacred, the medicinal and the aesthetic; it reflects life, earth, sky, nature, cosmos, the entire environment of life and living. It is the circle of life and death, old and new, youth and old age, the changing seasons. It is the Beautyway.

Connected with Nightway are both lore and ceremony. For

example, in Canyon de Chelly in Arizona, the Pueblo ruins referred to as House Made Of Dawn and White House are thought to be symbolic representations of Tsegihi, mentioned in Nightway as the dwelling place of the Sun. One of its principal heroes is Nayenezgani (Slayer Of Alien Gods or Monster Slayer), offspring of Father Sun and Mother Earth. The young god attempts to subdue and conquer evil, personified by the giants called Anaye who were the enemies of mankind.

That a race of giants existed some hundred thousand years ago is a subject of speculation among experts. But the discovery of fossil remains is an undeniable fact: skeletons six feet eight inches tall to seven feet eight inches tall have been unearthed in North Carolina (1874), California (1895), Death Valley (1898) and Wisconsin (1912). Lest one believes these to be isolated finds, consider the cemetery in northern Mexico (1930) where level upon level of corpses averaging eight feet in height were uncovered; and the seventeen-inch-long footprint found beside dinosaur tracks in Texas. Theoretically, these may be the Anaye whom the young war god was sent to slay.

Tribe leader. *See* Omaha, moral teaching.

Nez Perce

Chief Joseph. 1840 to 1904.

His parents were Khapkhaponimi (Bark Scrapings) and Tuekakas whom Joseph succeeded in 1873 as chief of the Wallamwatkin band of Nez Perce. He was born around 1840 in Oregon's Wallowa Valley and educated at the Lapwai Mission. His boyhood names were Hinmaton Yalatkit (Thunder Rolling In The Heights) and Ephraim—a baptismal name. Joseph, muscular and over six feet tall, an attractive man of enviable vitality and character was a peacemaker, not a warrior.

The Nez Perce is the only tribe known to selectively breed its equine stock. They developed the Appaloosa, which have broad chests and are swift racers with great stamina. Joseph's horse, Ebenezer, was the subject of newspaper articles whenever the chief rode into town. Demand for the powerful and attractive Appaloosa breed provided the people with a thriving, profitable horse trading economy.

In 1877, Chief Joseph was ordered to relocate his band to Idaho. Without informing their chief, some young braves, disheartened by the prejudice and inequities inflicted upon them, vented their frustrations in a final raid. Fearing reprisals, Joseph set a course for Canada to join Sitting Bull.

United States Army troops were deployed to pursue and return the frightened Nez Perce. There were only two hundred fighting men in his band, yet Chief Joseph outmarched and outmaneuvered ten different cavalry units, engaging in thirteen separate battles. His brilliant military strategies baffled the band's pursuers who dubbed him the "Indian Napoleon."

According to the army report, thinking he had crossed into Canada, Joseph stopped to rest his exhausted, starved people in northern Montana. They were overtaken by the military supposedly about thirty miles from the Canadian border. Some doubt this claim by the army and suspect that the cavalry entered Canada to capture the Nez Perce. Those who were strong enough to move on escaped and reached Sitting Bull's camp. But Chief Joseph remained with members too ill to continue their flight. Although enfeebled, they did not lack courage; even as the army charged the pathetic survivors, their determination to remain free was undiminished. The braves fought with that astounding superhuman strength known to surface when deep-rooted emotions are threatened. Historians refer to this infamous encounter as the Battle of Bear Paw. Near Chinook, Montana, Chief Joseph was arrested and sent to Oklahoma; the remainder of his band was taken to Idaho. After his release from prison, Joseph settled on the Colville Reservation in Washington Territory.

In tribute to Chief Joseph's exceptional qualities, a white marble monument was erected in the Nespelim Cemetery where he was buried in 1904.

Nisqualli

Janet McCloud. Contemporary.

Janet McCloud is the great-great-granddaughter of Chief Seattle. She is an Indian-rights activist associated with organizations formed to respond to Federal policy affecting native Americans, including treaty rights to fish waters of the Pacific

Northwest in Washington State. In dispute is the question of whether state codes take precedence over federally granted rights.

The issue of native American rights which Janet McCloud speaks about to audiences is not new. Chief Leschi led the last Nisqualli uprising against the United States Army in 1850 and was hanged for his heroic but futile attempt to retain tribal land rights. In the Treaty of Medicine Creek in 1854 and the Yakima Treaty of 1855, native Americans ceded all of their land except the reservation acreage in exchange for fishing rights in perpetuity.

Yakima Chiefs Meninock and Wallahee were tried in 1915 and found guilty of violating a state code on salmon fishing. The United States Army in 1918 confiscated 3943 acres of the 4700-acre Nisqualli reservation. In 1972, the army planned to expropriate the remaining 757 acres, once Chief Leschi's hunting grounds, for use as a training area and firing range. The commander of Ft. Lewis admitted in 1976 that the United States Army will probably fail in its attempt to seize the land because of Indian protests.

Nootka

Song to Bring Fair Weather. Ancient.

The Nootka live in the Pacific Northwest, mainly along the west coast of Vancouver Island, British Columbia. The Makah of Neah Bay, Washington, are the only Nootkan-speaking tribe in the United States. They are fishermen, some still use dugout canoes of ancient design, who live in long wooden houses and follow ancestral customs.

From the earliest remembered time, their fight for existence was a continuous struggle, and thoughts of death were remote; their primary concern was life. Love of life and indifference to death gave them a tranquility to be envied.

Nootkan philosophy was structured to allow for individualism in beliefs that were flexible and applicable to the needs of a people in an unpredictable environment. It was the unknown and unexplainable power of nature's spirits that caused them to fear and wonder. To these spirits they bowed in respect, as well as to the animals on whom they depended for sustenance. It required creativity for them to compose their songs on the spur of the moment, for spontaneous song composition is a conscious art which is at once unique, appropriate, heartfelt, and sincere.

Ojibwa

Shawondasee. Pre-Columbian.

Shawondasee means Southwind; this lodge tale characteristically conveys a moral intended to instruct and engross the listener. It was recorded in English for the first time around 1822. An adage among native Americans states that Indian summer, a short season of warm, hazy weather in the fall, comes to the northern hemisphere with its balmy, southern breezes when Shawondasee heaves a sigh.

Tribes of the New England region believed the warm breeze was the spirit of South Wind who provided their maize, beans and other blessings; he also cared for the souls of the dead. The Narragansetts called the spirit Canantowan.

The Little Spirit. Pre-Columbian.

This is one of a long list of lodge tales, part fact and part fiction, transmitted orally to each generation. Its origin has been traced to the Allegheny and Atlantic tribes and was recorded in English for the first time in 1839. *The Little Spirit* is sometimes titled *The Boy-Man;* it was used to teach a moral lesson.

The story evolves from the experiences of an orphan boy who is short in stature and doesn't grow tall as he grows older. It tells of his exploits in overcoming the condescension of others taller than he. By being self-confident and enterprising, he gains respect for his ability to perform tasks beyond the capability of those who previously ridiculed him.

White Feather. Flourished early 1900s.

The village of Lac du Flambeau (Lake of the Flaming Torch) is the center of the Chippewa (Ojibwa) Reservation in Wisconsin. Its name derives from an old Indian custom of fishing by torchlight. White Feather (Wabickigwun) lived there during the early 1900s, comforted by the high regard and respect accorded him. Both native Americans and whites admired his character traits and his observance of ancient traditions.

White Feather was a ceremony leader known as Kitci Odjanimwe Wegijig (Sky In Terrible Commotion). As a boy, he underwent a period of fasting during which he dreamed of a bird. In later years, he placed an image of the bird on a banner that fluttered from the medicine pole beside his dwelling.

White Feather was one of the delegates who carried two drums to the Menominee Reservation about a hundred and fifty miles from Lac du Flambeau. This ritual was part of the Drum-presentation ceremony. In that year, 1910, Wiskino (Bird) was chief of the Menominee West Branch Settlement near Shawano, Wisconsin.

In 1911, White Feather officiated at the Ceremony of Restoring the Mourners, marking the end of the mourning period for four Ojibwa; one was his aged mother whose husband, White Feather's father, had died.

Omaha

Ancient Ones. Ancient.

The Ancient Ones were responsible for establishing rituals and ceremonies that embodied their thoughts and conclusions on the relation of man to the All-Permeating Power. These prescribed ceremonies enabled the people to receive and benefit from the good gifts of the Power Above. The people show their gratitude to the Ancient Ones by representing them symbolically in ceremonies as a remembrance of their wisdom.

Big Elk. 1781 to 1853.

Big Elk (Ongpatonga), born around 1781, was a virile twenty-four-year-old brave living along the Missouri River near present-day Omaha, Nebraska, when the first white settlement was established at Bellevue in 1805. During the years that followed, he witnessed the white man's expansion into the Mississippi and lower Missouri valleys.

He had a wide-cheeked oval face and high forehead; his thin lips appeared sensuous beneath dreamy eyes that seemed to see beyond their immediate object of attention. Big Elk was broad-shouldered and muscular but did not flaunt his strength, for he was a refined man of high intellect.

Big Elk's oratorical skill made him an influential tribesman, often chosen to represent the people. He was attending a council at Portage des Sioux, Missouri, in 1815, when Chief Black Buffalo (Teton Sioux) died suddenly, and Black Elk addressed his poignant funeral oration to the mourners.

Big Elk represented the Omaha in Washington, D.C., in 1821 and 1837. Native Americans were brought to the Capital as part of the government's policy of intimidation by impressing them with the powers and wonders of white culture. The Omaha were lodged at George Miller's Tavern, an ill-famed hotel where slave dealers allegedly housed their "property" while traveling through the city. Big Elk and his fellow-tribesmen were outfitted in blue greatcoats trimmed with red cuffs, capes, and silver epaulettes. Blue trousers and black leather boots completed the costumes. Accessories included a hat designed in imitation of a coronet with blue and red bits of metal and feathers of bright colors, silver armbands, tomahawks, powder horns, and sheath knives.

Upon his return to Nebraska after the tour in 1821, Big Elk counciled with the people and told them his impressions of the dominant society. Hoping thereby, to help the people accept the changes he foresaw for them.

Chief Big Elk was a descendant of Chief Blackbird, for whom the Blackbird Hills were named. However, since his death in 1853, they have been known to the Omaha as "where Big Elk is buried."

Death song.

It was customary to show courage by singing a brave or death song at the moment of greatest danger or when death was imminent. The death song could be a public prayer or a private one between the singer and the Great Power Above. Sometimes the death song was received in a dream or vision; more often it was composed moments before death was expected. Each person devised his own song to convey what was most meaningful during his life, his expectations about the afterlife, or to impart a reckless disregard for the mortal consequences at hand. Singing the song with his final breath, the dying man expressed the urgency of the moment and self-control over his suffering.

Native Americans had many more occasions to sing death

songs after the advent of Europeans. Before that time, tribal wars were limited in duration and arms, but the white man's wars knew no season for death. However, it was not only in war that the death song was heard; native Americans aboard ships enroute to Europe frequently became seasick, then the death songs of many filled the air.

Estamaza. 1818 to 1888.

Estamaza (Iron Eyes) was also known as Joseph LaFlesche, born around 1818, the son of a French fur trader and an Osage woman named Waoowinchtcha.

In 1843, he married Hinnuaganun (The One Woman) whose maiden name was Mary Gale; she was the daughter of Dr. John Gale and Nicomi whose father was an Iowa chief. Mary Gale mothered Susette, a lecturer and spokeswoman for Indian rights; Rosalie and Marguerite who were educators; and Susan, a physician graduated from Women's Medical College of Pennsylvania in 1889.

Following tribal custom, Estamaza took a second wife, Elizabeth Esau, more familiarly called Tainne. She became the mother of Zhogaxe (Woodworker), known professionally as Francis LaFlesche. He earned a degree in jurisprudence but is best known for his work as a writer and anthropologist.

Estamaza was as remarkable as the children he sired. He spoke French, Omaha, Sioux, Iowa, Pawnee, and Oto. Big Elk, shortly before his death, chose dynamic Estamaza to succeed him as chief of the Omaha.

Although one of his legs had been partially amputated and the stump fitted with a prosthesis made of cork, Estamaza was very active. Making frequent rounds of the reservation, he assessed changes needed to improve the lives of the people. He established a village patterned after a white settlement, laid out roads, set aside land for cultivation, and planted the first wheat on the reservation. All of the children attended mission school so they could compete on equal terms with white neighbors. Estamaza hired white carpenters to build his house and instructed tribe members to observe the techniques of construction. The knowledge thus acquired, enabled them to erect small houses for themselves.

Estamaza died in 1888, the last of the Omaha chiefs.

Ethic. *See* Omaha, moral teaching.

Hethu'shka Society tenet. Pre-Columbian.

The Hethu'shka Society was established to foster heroic acts and a disdain for the fear of death; it inspired its members with the highest ideals of courage and bravery. The society tempered the warriors' zeal by reminding them that man must conform his acts to the wills of the gods, for only the Thunder gods had the power to decree who would die.

Each of the society's one hundred or more songs commemorate a historical incident or was composed to assist its members in recollecting their duties.

Because the society allowed its songs to be used by non-members, its teachings spread throughout the Omaha tribe and rapidly became a standard of conduct. Its rules encouraged peace and harmony within the tribe and its beneficial influence was quickly recognized and adopted in some variation by the Osage, Iowa, Oto, Pawnee, Sioux, and Winnebago tribes.

Introduction of the Child to the Cosmos. Pre-Columbian.

When a child was born, the parents notified the clan that had custody of the rite. The ceremony of introduction took place on the eighth day after birth, when the priest was invited to the lodge of the infant's parents. Cradling the babe in his left arm, the priest approached the lodge door. In the entranceway, he stood facing East and raised his right hand, palm upward to the sky, then cried out in a loud, ringing voice his petition on behalf of the child.

The supplication is steeped in antiquity and is reminiscent of a time predating established rites and ceremonies as it intones the Omaha belief in the oneness of all life forms and the four levels of human development: Infancy, Youth, Adulthood, and Old Age.

Moral teaching.

Moral and ethical principles, based on accepted standards of right and wrong, governed the people's conduct and sense of duty and justice. In each tribe, there was a small group devoted to musing upon human relationships in philosophical and metaphysical terms, defining and redefining their conclusions as their knowledge increased. They combined secular, priestly and mystical activities; the wisdom thus obtained was imparted to the people and conveyed orally to succeeding generations. These were the Wise Men, the Old Ones, the sages who attributed their insight to meditation and interpretation of reality as reflected in human experience and in nature. All good that accrued to the tribe was ascribed to collective discrimination of changes affecting the people.

It was believed that a desirable result could be achieved through individual meditation and will-power. Therefore, emphasis was placed upon personal contemplation of observable events. Self-reliance and strength of character were highly valued in an individual. The attributes expected of men were courage, fortitude, generosity and fidelity; women were expected to be industrious, hospitable, faithful, and fruitful. Custom favored those who could be relied on to perform their duties without continuous supervision. Societal ridicule was a powerful incentive to conform.

Oral tradition. *See* Omaha, moral teaching.

Proverb. *See* Apache, proverb.

Social etiquette. *See* Omaha, moral teaching.

To Weep For Loss. Ancient.

In the Omaha language, this prayer is called *Wakonda gikon.* It is recited to evoke compassion from the mysterious power while the vision-seeker stands alone in a quiet place, testing his endurance. With utmost humility, the All-Permeating Life-Force is beseeched; the supplicant confesses his dependence on a power higher than himself and summons aid from Wakonda to help fill the void that caused the seeker to utter his prayer.

This rite could be performed in solitude by one person, in contrast to most other rites which involve the entire tribe.

Wawan Ceremony. Ancient.

Wawan means "To sing for someone." This refers to the singing which accompanies the two ceremonial pipes. The eagle is a central figure of the ceremony, therefore, seven tail feathers of a golden eagle, in addition to the pipes, are the main articles used during the ceremony.

The rite commemorates the conclusion of a peace treaty between the Omaha, Ponca, Cheyenne, Arikara and other tribes. For this reason, the Wawan Ceremony is performed with joyful spirit in keeping with its theme of peace, symbolically rendered by reference to a "clear sky," that is, free of storm clouds, with the connotation of freedom from war and its disturbing effects.

Most of its songs consist of vocables representing lyrics that are now lost. The vocables were deliberately substituted for the original words in the distant past to keep them secret and known only to the priests. Its performance becomes a binding link and reminder of the obligations incurred by the tribes who made the treaty.

Onondaga

Canasateego. Flourished early to mid-1700s.

Bold and enterprising, Canasateego was a powerful chief of the Five Nations Iroquois Confederacy who played an important role in council proceedings at Philadelphia, Pennsylvania, in 1742. The assembly was called to mediate a land dispute between white settlers and the Delaware tribe. The Europeans satisfactorily proved they had paid for the land, therefore, the chiefs of the confederacy ruled in their favor.

Canasateego tempered his pragmatism with a sense of humor. During a meeting in 1744, an English officer boasted of a recent victory over the French army. The chief replied, "Well, if that be the case, you must have taken a great deal of rum from them, and can afford to give us some, that we may rejoice with you." Glasses were soon raised in a victory toast.

Canasateego had a son named Hans Jacob who resided by the Ohio River in 1758.

Papago

Anonymous tribesman. *See* Eskimo, anonymous.

Pawnee

Ancient holy man. Ancient.

Tribal holy men, or priests as they were sometimes called, were ever conscious of their duty to the people and sought examples in nature to clarify their teachings.

The *Song of the Wren* was composed in the very distant past by a priest who used it to show that happiness and joy are possible for everyone, even the most humble. The idea occurred to him after listening to the ecstatic trilling of a wren. Although it is one of the smallest and least powerful among birds, it is a merry creature whose song is incredibly melodious and joyful. The association of thoughts inspired the holy man to teach a very profound lesson: the value of life is in the living, all else is unimportant.

Death song. *See* Omaha, death song.

Hako, fifteenth ritual. Ancient.

Prior to and during the 17th century, the *Hako* ceremony was observed by tribes of a vast geographical area. Tradition indicates that it may have come from the Caddoan tribe which guided Francisco Vasquez de Coronado in 1541 during his search for the city of Quivira. Some authorities believe it may be the rite described by Jacques Marquette after his visit to the now extinct Illinois tribe in 1672. The *Hako* is strikingly similar to the Eleusinian Mysteries of ancient Attica in Greece.

About twenty principal rituals are embodied in the *Hako*, which can be performed in spring, summer and fall, but never during winter. The Kurahus Tahirussawichi explained that the *Hako* expressed the belief that there is above us a holy place to which man can address his prayers. It is the place where Tirawa the Creator lives. The teachings of the *Hako* can be thought of as a direct link to Tirawa; if conscientiously observed, man is assured of receiving the spiritual help he asks for. It also affirms the Pawnee belief in an orderly and harmonious universe.

The Kurahus.

"Kurahus" is the conventional title used to address a Pawnee priest; it is usually preceded by "the" and is comparable to "Reverend" or "Father" when addressing the clergy in English. The Kurahus is the conductor of a ceremony, and for his service, custom obligated him to levy a fee. Typically, he received two ponies as gifts from children participating in the lengthy *Hako* ceremony.

A tangible gift was also required from an apprentice priest to insure his appreciation of the value of the knowledge imparted by the Kurahus. This was a very serious undertaking for the apprentice and his instructor because many years were needed to learn the rites and songs. They spent long hours together in prayer and studying the meanings of the rituals to preserve them exactly as their forebears knew and taught them.

The Kurahus, *Hako, Birth of Dawn. See* Pawnee, *Hako,* fifteenth ritual.

The Kurahus Tahirussawichi. 1828 to ?

He was a full-blood Chaui-Pawnee ceremonial leader born around 1828. In the years 1898 and 1900, the Kurahus traveled to Washington, D.C., to record the songs of the *Hako* and to explain their significance within the ceremony. He was past the age of seventy at the time and extremely fearful of revealing what up to then had been a rite never before performed in its entirety for anyone other than native Americans. He preceded and ended each session with Alice C. Fletcher of the American Bureau of Ethnology by praying to Tirawa for guidance to correctly perform the ritual and to bless the project.

The Kurahus Tahirussawichi was a man of utmost good will, a holy man in every sense. Many have expressed gratitude for his contribution to an understanding of this deeply moving ceremony.

Oral teaching. *See* Omaha, moral teaching.

Pima

Advice from a father. *See* Oglala Sioux, village elder.

Ethic. *See* Cherokee, ethic.

George Webb. 1893 to ____.
   George Webb, also known as Buzzing Feather, was born
around 1893 on the Gila River Reservation at Gila Crossing,
Arizona, where the family's farm was situated. This section is
now called Santa Cruz Village. His mother was Rainbow's Ends
and his father was Kelihi (Old Fashioned), the son of Eagle-
feathers and Juana Losso.
   Webb labored as a ranch-hand and farm manager. At age
twenty-eight he married, purchased livestock and became an
independent cattle rancher and farmer. Agriculture by irrigation,
a system developed by the Hohokam as early as 400 B.C., is used
in this region, but after a long dry-spell, Webb was forced to
abandon farming. Eventually, he also sold his cattle. Nevertheless, he continued to live on his thirty-acre farm, supporting his
family by operating a grocery store.
   In 1934, he represented Gila Crossing residents at the first
Tribal Council, and in 1942, was appointed associate Judge of the
Tribal Court—a post he held until 1950. Two of his sons are
armed service veterans; one served in Europe, the other in Korea.
   In his book, *A Pima Remembers*, Webb tells of Pima history
and traditions as they relate to his own experience with them in a
modern age. He writes with a witty and sometimes biting humor
overlaid with good natured warmth and understanding.

Potawatomi

Metea. 1781 to ?
   The Potawatomi had occupied both sides of Lake Michigan
in Indiana and Illinois long before Metea's birth around 1781. The
years of his youth were turbulent times for the tribe; its warriors
fought in support of Little Turtle's campaigns, and in the battle of
Fallen Timbers.
   In the War of 1812, when the Potawatomi sided with the
British, Metea was already a battle-tested warrior. His income

included a pension from the British crown for his services.

Chief Metea left his village near the Wabash in 1821 to attend a council in Chicago to discuss terms of a land purchase desired by Euro-Americans. Metea's appearance was very impressive: tall and slender, dignified in manner, sparkling black eyes that reflected sincerity, and the resonant voice of a seasoned orator. People took little notice of his withered arm, the result of a severe wound sustained in battle at Ft. Wayne in Indiana.

Though vehemently against the sale of additional tribal land, he addressed the assembly of three thousand people with a conciliatory attitude and presented a facetious, well-reasoned and fair evaluation of the territorial "needs" of his people as opposed to the "wants" of white settlers.

Powhatan

Wahunsonacock (Powhatan). 1547 to 1622.

Wahunsonacock, alternately called Mamanatowick (Great King) and Ottaniack, was principal chief of the Powhatan Confederacy, an alliance of thirty to forty Algonquian-speaking tribes. Powhatan villages extended along the James River near Richmond, Virginia, where Wahunsonacock was born around 1547. Powhatan is a place and tribe name, but Captain John Smith assumed it was the chief's name and this error has been preserved in history books.

When Smith met him in 1607, Wahunsonacock was a tall, well-proportioned, exceedingly vigorous man with long, gray hair and a sad countenance. A racoonskin robe and feather headdress fashioned to resemble a crown added to his dignified appearance. Forty to fifty tall braves accompanied him on travels and four were posted to stand at each corner of his house when he occupied it. At mealtimes, Wahunsonacock was attended by his wives; before and after meat was served, one of them brought a wooden bowl of water to cleanse his hands, another waited with a cluster of feathers with which to dry them. He had many wives, but the names of only thirteen of his favorites have been recorded. In 1609, he had about twenty living sons and more than ten daughters; two of his daughters were named Cleopatra and Pocahontas.

Wahunsonacock ruled by "consent of the governed." Under his leadership, the confederacy increased in both size and power. Werowocomoco (Chief Place Of Council), on the Pamunkey (Where We Took A Sweat Bath) River, was its capital and the chief's main residence. However, Wahunsonacock disliked having colonists nearby—Jamestown was about fifteen miles away—so he moved to the more distant Orapax, which is now Hanover County, Virginia.

Insensitive to the chief's sylvan habitat, Captain Smith imposed European customs on Wahunsonacock's position as head of the confederacy by arranging a coronation ceremony in 1609. King James of England sent a copper crown, scarlet cloak, a huge ornate bed, and other furniture and objects equally useless. Wahunsonacock stored them in a temple dedicated to the god Cakeres, where his ancestors were buried.

Smith placed outrageously high value on items he traded with native Americans. In one transaction, he demanded, besides a variety of articles, a large section of land in exchange for two guns and a grinding stone. The chief was aware of the inequity of the trades, but in sympathy for the starving settlers, he continued to bring them agricultural products harvested by his people.

During the twenty-two years that followed Wahunsona-cock's death in 1622, less tolerant leaders undertook a series of hostile actions against the colonists in an attempt to force their removal. One of them was Opechancanough who was almost one hundred years old when the English captured him in 1644. He was unceremoniously hauled into Jamestown where he was shot and killed by a guard.

Sauk

Black Hawk. 1767 to 1838.

His father, Pyesa, emigrated from Montreal, Canada, to settle in the Sauk village called Saukenuk, present-day Rock Island, Illinois, where Black Hawk was born in 1767. He was called Makataimeshekiakiak (Black Sparrow Hawk); the mother of his three children was Singing Bird (Asshewequa).

People of his tribe described the chief as tall, handsome, kindhearted, and of an amiable disposition. He allied with

Tecumseh and served as Brevet Brigadier General in the British army in the War of 1812. Black Hawk's animosity toward Euro-Americans stemmed from his contention that the Treaty of 1804, ceding the entire State of Illinois and part of Missouri and Wisconsin, was invalid. Some modern historians agree with his interpretation.

It is clear from military reports and civilian accounts that cavalry officers were unable to restrain their men. The Sauk were shot on sight. Black Hawk and other tribesmen were beaten and robbed; the women were assaulted by white neighbors who trespassed on tribal land to do so. While the band was away on its winter hunt, the lodges were occupied by whites, personal possessions confiscated, and the land plowed up.

Black Hawk's attempt to regain tribal property is referred to as The Black Hawk War of 1832. Arrayed against him were men destined to become politically prominent: Captain Abraham Lincoln, Colonel Zachary Taylor and Lieutenant Jefferson Davis; future Illinois governors Thomas Ford, Joseph Duncan and Thomas Carlin; Henry Dodge who became Governor of Wisconsin; and Orville Browning who was elected Senator and later became Secretary of the Interior.

One aspect that doomed Black Hawk's hope for success was the ingrained moral training of native Americans to tell the truth. Whenever the United States military questioned captured warriors, their honesty often divulged Black Hawk's strategies. He made several attempts at reconciliation, but each time his men approached the cavalry under a white flag, they were killed before they could explain their mission. Black Hawk survived the decisive battle at Bad Axe River in Wisconsin, but was apprehended later and imprisoned at Jefferson Barracks near St. Louis, Missouri.

He was released in 1833, then taken to Washington, D.C., to confer with government authorities; he was in the Capital again in 1837 during a tour of Eastern cities. Black Hawk met with President Andrew Jackson who gave him an ornate sword and uniform; Henry Clay gifted him with a cane and John Quincy Adams presented him with a medal. All of these became part of Black Hawk's funeral attire upon his death in 1838 at his home on the Des Moines River near Iowaville, Iowa.

The chief's body was placed in a seated position and interred according to ancient burial rites. The grave was desecrated the following winter; the skeleton was traced to Quincy, Illinois, where it had been sent to be wired together. It was consumed in an 1855 fire which destroyed the Burlington Geographical and Historical Society Museum in Iowa.

Seneca

Cornplanter. 1736 to 1836.

He was light-skinned and his mother told him that his father was John O'Bail, a white man residing in Albany, New York. Cornplanter, born around 1736 in a village on the Genessee River in New York, was called Gyantwaka (By What One Plants).

Cornplanter held a well-regarded position in the tribe until 1789 when he was responsible for ceding a large tract of land at Ft. Harmar, Ohio. For this, he was severely ostracized by his people; in 1790, he asked Congress to review and reconsider all treaties with the Seneca. To placate Cornplanter, the Federal Government awarded him a pension for his cooperation, and in 1796, the State of Pennsylvania gave him a land grant along the Allegheny River in Warren County for his personal reservation. He allocated half of the land to use by other Seneca; nevertheless, those who had been dispossessed by the treaties he had negotiated continued to harass him until he became embittered by the lack of concern for his predicament from the dominant society. Cornplanter was still seeking a resolution of the problem when he and Red Jacket went to Washington, D.C., in 1823 and again in 1827.

The beleagered chief died at Cornplanter Village, or Obale-town as it was also known, and was buried on the reservation. Cornplanter regretted his misplaced trust in Euro-Americans during his lifetime, but the final thrust of insult was still in the future. In 1960, the reservation and his grave were flooded when the Kinzua dam was built.

Twylah Nitsch. Contemporary.

Twylah Nitsch belongs to the Seneca Wolf Clan; her ancestors include Red Jacket. She and her husband, Bob, have four children and live on the Cattaraugus Reservation in New York where she was born.

She is a woman of many talents and diversified interests. Nitsch's delightful children's clan stories are an extension of her career as an educator. She has taught at Rosary Hill College in Buffalo, New York, but some of her most creative teaching skills become evident during classes conducted in the Cattaraugus longhouse. This is also the meeting-place of the Seneca Indian Historical Society which she and her mother, Maude Shongo Hurd, established in 1970. Buildings on the reservation near Buffalo include the home her great-grandfather, Two Guns, built in 1858.

A visionary and mystic, she teaches ancient Seneca philosophy as she learned it from her grandfather, Moses Shongo. Nitsch's commitment to its preservation is an example to students of self-discipline through will-power. Emphasizing individual spiritual development, she teaches that locked within each seeker's own being is a secret source of great medicine. Those who discover it through the Pathway of Peace, find wisdom and illumination that results in self-realization.

Arthur C. Parker. 1881 to 1955.

Arthur C. Parker was born to a distinguished family at Iroquois, Cattaraugus Reservation, New York. His mother was a Scots-English woman named Geneva Griswold. His father, Frederick Parker, was a descendant of a founder of the Iroquois Confederacy and of Handsome Lake, the prophet whose *Code of Handsome Lake* Arthur C. Parker translated and published. He was also a great-nephew of General Ely S. Parker, a United States Army officer and the first native American Commissioner of Indian Affairs. Adopted by the Bear Clan in ancient ritual, he was named Gawasowaneh (Big Snowsnake) and initiated into the most sacred tribal organization, the Little Water Society.

Parker attended Harvard University in Massachusetts and became a field archaeologist for its Peabody Museum in 1903. From 1906 to 1911, he was an archaeologist for the New York State Museum in Albany. He was director of the Rochester Museum of Arts and Sciences from 1925 to 1946. Parker received an honorary Master of Science degree from the University of Rochester in 1922; an honorary Doctorate in Science from Union College in 1940; and Keuka College honored him with the

Doctorate of Humane Laws in 1945. He was chosen for the Indian Council Fire Award in 1936.

Educated and imbued with native American traditions, Parker had three hundred fifty titles published, fourteen were books about North American Indians. With forty-three other college educated native Americans, he founded and was President of the Society of American Indians; he was editor of its quarterly journal from 1911 to 1916. Parker died in 1955 at Naples, New York, a world-renowned museum curator.

Red Jacket. 1756 to 1830.

Seneca County, New York, probably at Canoga, was the place of Red Jacket's birth around 1756. He was then called Otetiani (Always Ready), but when elected chief, he acquired the name Shagoiewatha (He Who Causes Them To Be Awake). Both names aptly described his character.

Red Jacket was tall and slender with a patrician bearing, and naturally inclined toward a mild temperament; but he attacked the despoiling effects of white culture with vehement oratory. Yet, he maintained a grace and dignity that added force to his denunciations.

In a clear, animated voice, Red Jacket once defended himself successfully for three uninterrupted hours before a tribal council at Buffalo Creek, New York, in response to Cornplanter's accusation of cowardice. He not only saved his life thereby, but also gained admirers and a reputation as one of the greatest orators of his day.

Red Jacket's phenomenal memory, expert horsemanship and stamina as a long distance runner, were invaluable to the English who employed him as a messenger. Of the uniform they gave him, he showed a preference for the red jacket and made it part of his regular attire long after his association with the English ended. As a result, he was identified as Red Jacket. He understood English but refused to speak it, replying only after an interpreter translated the words into his own language.

Red Jacket met with President George Washington in 1792 and received an oval silver medal; similar medals given to native Americans in subsequent years were alluded to as "Red Jacket medals."

During the early 1800s, Red Jacket lived in a log cabin on the

Seneca Reservation near Buffalo, New York. He was accused of leading a "pagan" faction which opposed entry on tribal land to Christian missionaries, but his intent was to preserve native American culture from white inroads. Sensing imminent death, Red Jacket visited relatives and friends, discussing with them the current condition of the Seneca and relating, as far back as his knowledge extended, the tribe's history. When he died in 1830, funeral rites were performed in the mission church; he was buried on a parcel of land owned by the Wolf Clan to which he belonged. In 1884, Red Jacket was reburied in Forest Lawn cemetery at Buffalo, New York.

Moses Shongo. Flourished mid-1800s to early 1900s.
    Shongo means "In the water (or spring)." In young adulthood, Moses Shongo moved from the Buffalo Creek Reservation at Allegany to the Cattaraugus Reservation near Buffalo, New York. Here, he met and married the daughter of Jane and Daniel Webster Pierce; Pierce was an educator in local schools. Shongo and his bride dressed in fashions typical of the 1800s; their reservation home was patterned after those found in the nearby white community. However, they lived according to the philosophy of Shongo's ancestors. At the time, he was the last of the practicing Seneca teacher-priests, a fact which troubled him deeply.
    In time, his daughter, Maude Shongo Hurd, gave birth to an infant destined to carry on his work. Shongo began explaining tribal philosophy to his granddaughter, Twylah, when she was still a child. Seneca wisdom, rooted in an understanding of human nature and spiritual needs, is perpetuated by Twylah Hurd Nitsch at Shongo Farms on the Cattaraugus Reservation.

Shawnee

Thomas Wildcat Alford. 1860 to 1938.
    He was born in 1860 in a village by the Canadian River in Seminole County, Oklahoma. His childhool name was Gaynwawpiahsika (One Of long Following). His father's name was Wildcat, a transliteration of Gaytahkipiahsikah (Lying Spotted In The Brush). Alford's mother was an Absentee Shawnee named

Waylahskise (Graceful One), the great-granddaughter of Tecumseh. Thomas Wildcat Alford was educated in mission schools until 1879 when he entered Hampton Institute in Hampton, Virginia, where he converted to Christianity.

After his return from Virginia, Alford taught in and became principal of a reservation school. Later, he was employed as a land surveyor and interpreter. He and his wife, Mary Grinnell, had five children.

Alford was instrumental in easing the people's transition from accustomed practice to conformity with contradictory Federal decrees. Private land ownership was particularly perplexing, so Alford impressed upon them the value of registering for a land allotment, but many abhorred the idea. This sentiment was exploited by whites who purchased the allotments for paltry sums. On occasion, Alford forestalled such sales, but the acreage deeded to settlers reached alarming proportions. He pleaded in Washington, D.C., for Federal restraints, but political expediency doomed his attempt to failure.

To preserve the Shawnee language, Alford translated the gospels of the New Testament. The work was titled *The Four Gospels Of Our Lord Jesus Christ* and published in 1929. He also authored *Civilization,* an eyewitness account of the opening and settlement of Oklahoma from the time it was Indian Territory, the sanctuary for some thirty displaced tribes, to its statehood. Alford died in 1938 at Shawnee, Oklahoma.

Tecumseh. 1768 to 1813.

Tecumseh was born around 1768 in Piqua (Town That Rises From The Ashes) near Springfield, Ohio. He was the son of Shawnee Chief Puckenshinwa (I Light From Flying) and Methoataske (A Turtle Laying Her Eggs In The Sand) who belonged to either the Cherokee or Creek tribe. It has been variously stated that Tecumseh, the fifth of eight children, was a triplet—the others being Lalawéthika (who became the prophet Tenskwatawa) and Kumskaka.

Between 1807 and 1813, Tecumseh (One Who Passes Across Intervening Space From One Point To Another) was known as the prophet Shooting Star, a variant allusion to his name. Writers of his time describe Tecumseh as almost six feet tall, courtly in

carriage and of very high character, readily admitting being wrong
and extending an apology. Contemporaries frequently com-
mented about his revulsion to vengeful cruelty and his self-
control. He was pensive and persevering, but quickly denounced
injustices perpetrated by white settlers. Tecumseh was not
ostentatious; however, his clothing became his trademark—a
white buckskin shirt, beaded leggings and a feather-tipped blue-
and-red headband.

At age twenty-eight, he married Manete; they had one child,
a son called Pugeshashenwa (A Panther In The Act Of Seizing Its
Prey). Rebecca Galloway, a white woman, taught Tecumseh to
speak English by reading Shakespearean plays and history books.
He was a Brigadier General in the British army during the War
of 1812.

Tecumseh and The Open Door established Prophet Town at
the junction of Tippecanoe Creek and the Wabash River in
Indiana. Working toward a confederacy, Tecumseh spoke to the
assembled populations of many tribes. During his visit to the
Upper Creek Nation in Tahabatchi (Elmore County, Alabama),
Big Warrior, an influential member of the tribe council, expressed
doubt that Tecumseh's mission was divinely inspired. Reacting
with dramatic flair to support the truth of his statements,
Tecumseh predicted that when he reached Ft. Detroit in
Michigan Territory, he would stamp his foot and the earth would
tremble, shaking down the houses in Big Warrior's village. On the
day that Tecumseh would have been expected to arrive at his
distination, a deep rumbling was heard in Tahabatchi. Frightened
villagers ran from their homes shouting, "Tecumseh has arrived
in Detroit."

It is a historical fact that around that time (December 1811),
the first recorded earthquake in North America occurred at New
Madrid, Missouri. Tremors, felt throughout the lower half of the
continent, leveled every building within an area of fifty thousand
square miles.

Tecumseh sustaind a mortal head wound in 1813 during the
Battle of the Thames near Chatham, in Ontario, Canada. He was
buried near the site of his death.

Wampum Belt message. Ancient.
This particular wampum belt was delivered by a Shawnee

messenger to the Cherokee as part of a Seneca-inspired plan to establish peace among the Seneca, Cherokee, Shawnee, and Wyandot tribes. The belt was first read to a peace council at Tahlequah, present-day Tellico Plains, Tennessee. It had been handed down through many generations before it was read again to eighteen tribes assembled at the new Cherokee capital, Tahlequah, Indian Territory in 1843. John Ross was the presiding officer, assisted by Major George Lowery, second in authority to Ross. At that time, it was thought that Major Lowery was the only Cherokee still able to read the wampum belt and interpret its historical record.

Shoshone

Washakie. 1804 to 1900.

Pinquana (Sweet Smelling), as he was called, was born around 1804. He lived among his mother's people, the Eastern Shoshone who occupied parts of Utah and Wyoming along the Green River. His father, Paseego, belonged to the Umatilla tribe. Historians identify him as Washakie (Gourd Rattle), but after becoming chief of the Eastern Shoshone in 1843, tribesmen referred to him as "White-haired chief with scarred face."

Because Euro-Americans outnumbered them in manpower and arms, Washakie reasoned that the Shoshone could gain more from cooperating with the Federal Government than resisting white culture. Therefore, he counseled his people to live in peace. During treaty negotiations in 1868, he demanded and got Wind River Valley in Wyoming as a settlement site. Before signing the agreement, he read it thoroughly to assure himself of the government's agreement "in writing" to the school, instructors, church, mill, hospital, farm implements, seed, and army post which he had stipulated as conditions for obtaining his signature.

The Shoshone settled in the Owl Creek, Wind River, and Sweetwater sections. Later, it was discovered that the Sweetwater gold mines lay partly within the reservation; an influx of miners followed the golden lure. Thousands crowded into the area and, predictably, the reservation was opened to white pioneers in 1905. Washakie still advised against armed resistence and joined the Episcopal Church as an example of his own commitment. As a token of his friendship and service with military forces, President Ulysses S. Grant gave him an ornate silver-decorated saddle.

Washakie died in 1900 while visiting in Montana; he was buried with military honors at Ft. Washakie in Wyoming.

Sioux

Anecdote. Self-explanatory.

Bad Arm. Flourished 1800s.

Bad Arm was troubled for many years with an old injury to his elbow and this may account for his name. He came from a family of illustrious men who traced their ancestry through those who bore the name Man Afraid Of His Horse. With Crazy Horse and Sitting Bull, Bad Arm shared those tension-filled years which bore the brunt of the Federal Megastructure and its monopoly over the lives of native Americans. He was one of the few to survive the Wounded Knee Creek Massacre in 1890, but his wife and children were killed and he never forgot the tragedy. Bad Arm was a friendly person who loved children and paid them much attention. The birth of his grandson, Young One, was a joyful event.

He liked to reminisce about the past to the rhythm of a drum; at such times, he recalled the carefree, happy days along the Powder and Tongue rivers—those days before Bad Arm came to live on the reservation at Pine Ridge, South Dakota.

Buffalo Child Long Lance. 1893 to _____.

It is said that Chief Buffalo Child Long Lance is a "Croatan Negro" named Sylvester Long, born in North Carolina in 1893. His autobiography is a sensitive account of Siouan life on the northern plains, where he lived at the time it was written. In the past, the Sioux occupied vast tracts of land West of the Mississippi and sections of the Appalachian Mountains in Virginia, North Carolina, and South Carolina. According to traditions of the Lumbee (in Robeson County, North Carolina), who claim descent from the Croatan, the fabled "Lost Colony" English survivors intermarried with the Croatan, migrated southward, and joined with Eastern Sioux bands.

One method colonists used to rid the continent of its native owners, was to sell them overseas as slaves, replacing them with Black slaves who had no claim to the land. The first Black slaves arrived in the colonies in 1619. Consequently, the colonization of North America is intertwined with the histories of native American and Black races.

Crispus Attucks, first victim of the American Revolution in 1770, was the son of a Black man and a Massachuset woman named Ahtuk (A Small Deer)—from which his surname derived. Examples of Indian-Black integration are common to many tribes.

Contrary's widow. Flourished 1800s.

She married a Heyoka, the traditional Contrary. Their courtship had been a stop-go, yes-no affair, for the Contrary, according to instructions received in his dream, was always required to say the opposite of what he intended. Her spontaneous smile, happy laughter, and good humor encouraged her husband in his arduous role. The Heyoka is a clown who has received the most powerful vision possible: the Thunder Being. He is many but only one; he is shapeless, yet he has wings; he is devoid of feet but his talons are long and sharp; although he is headless, his beak is long; his voice is the sound of thunder, and the glance of his eye is lightning.

Contrary and his wife were contemporaries of Bad Arm and lived on the Pine Ridge Reservation in South Dakota. After her husband died, she went to live with her granddaughter. Contrary's widow, dressed in calico and puffing on a short-stemmed pipe as she sat in the wagon, accompanied the young woman on her honeymoon.

Oral tradition. *See* Omaha, moral teaching.

Proverb. *See* Apache, proverb.

Wilbur Riegert. Contemporary.

Wilbur Riegert is a contemporary Sioux troubled by the extent of poverty on reservations and the destruction of family life resulting from oppressive government programs. He is addressing the same problems discerned by Crazy Horse and Sitting Bull, among others, who are famed in North American history mainly for their war exploits. It is unjust to perpetuate such characterizations without revealing their basic cause: the right to be free men in a country that prides itself on the liberty of its people.

Since 1832, almost every facet of native American life has been directed by the Bureau of Indian Affairs, and reinforced by state and city bureaucracies into modern times. In *The New Haven Register* on December 30, 1976, Jack Anderson said: "Today, an unpublished congressional report declares, state and local authorities continue to erode the proud Indian heritage by breaking up families.

"The report, based on a lengthy investigation by the American Indian Review Commission, states that social welfare officials disrupt Indian society by removing children from their families and placing them in non-Indian foster homes."

Marquis Childs, writing in the New Haven *Journal-Courier* on June 28, 1979, stated: "The great majority of the Sioux live on reservations in South Dakota, and their plight could hardly be worse. Unemployment runs from seventy to eighty percent and gainful work is often nonexistent."

Some native Americans have attempted assimilation into white culture and succeeded; others have failed. Unable to make the transition, they live in ghettos such as those in Chicago, Los Angeles, and Omaha.

Social ethic. *See* Cherokee, ethic.

Tribe elder. *See* Oglala Sioux, village elder.

Village wise man. *See* Oglala Sioux, village elder.

Warcaziwin. Contemporary.

Around 1930, Warcaziwin (Sunflower) of the Sioux tribe, addressed a gathering during ceremonies observing the U.S. flag raising over the Pio Pico California State Historic Monument. The adobe mansion near Whittier, California, was the residence of the last Mexican Governor of California. Its vast acreage once extended outward to El Camino Real (The Royal Road), developed during Spanish occupancy.

Warcaziwin's presence lent substance to the shadow of Indian culture that overlays the land and reflected in her spirited sense of pride. Foreign intrusions affected native Americans in varying ways, but their imprint is always found beside the invader's. El Camino Real connects missions built by Spanish Padre Junipero Serra, but they bear the indelible mark of their native converts. Wall paintings in several missions are the works of native American artists dating back to 1798. Santa Barbara and San Miguel Arcangel come alive to throbbing drums and colorful costumes during annual dance festivals on mission grounds. Christian native Americans living in the valley still worship at Mission Santa Ines.

Brulé Sioux

Spotted Tail. 1824 to 1881.

The Brulé Sioux lived in the White River area of South Dakota when Spotted Tail was born around 1824. He was called Jumping Buffalo, formerly the name of his father, a Blackfoot of the Saone Band, known as Cunka (Tangle Hair). His mother was Walks With The Pipe, a Brulé.

Spotted Tail (Sinte Gleska) matured to robust manhood. Having counted twenty-six coups at a very early age, he was regarded a great warrior. He was also often called Speaks To The Woman because he had a reputation for flirting.

When negotiating with white authorities, Spotted Tail preferred friendly persuasion rather than force. The goodnatured, but shrewd leader of the Ring Band was elected principal chief in 1866. At this time, he drew a government salary for acting as liaison between the tribe and United States agents. Spotted Tail insisted on being paid in one dollar bills which he distributed to poor families. Additionally, the government spent eight thousand dollars to build a house for him. Spotted Tail could read and write English.

With others, he was delegated to negotiate mineral rights in the Black Hills with Federal agencies in Washington, D.C. The Sioux refused an offer of six million dollars; Spotted Tail had interviewed knowledgeable men about the value of the minerals and knew their true worth.

To gain control of the Black Hills, Congress passed a law in 1877 which in effect abrogated an important requirement in an 1868 treaty. In June 1979, the U.S. Court of Claims ruled favorably on an award of seventeen and a half million dollars for the land and between ninety and one hundred fifteen million dollars interest at five percent for the hundred and two years during which the principal remained unpaid. Compensation for the seizure was jeopardized when six months later, Federal attorneys contested the interest award before the Supreme Court.

Turbulence within and without the tribe during the latter 1800s, a period of transition for the people, saw minor grievances inflated to intense emotional outbursts that culminated in Spotted Tail's death in 1881. He was shot by Crow Dog near Big Turkey camp on the Rosebud Reservation in South Dakota and buried in the Episcopal cemetery. His son, William Spotted Tail, succeeded him as chief.

Hunkpapa Sioux

Black Moon. Flourished 1800s.

Chief Black Moon, a Hunkpapa Sioux who flourished during the 1800s was distinguished for his courage and integrity. He was a confidant of Sitting Bull and rode with him in 1868 to meet Father Pierre Jean De Smet, and delivered the welcoming speech when they later formally convened in council.

After Sitting Bull was elected principal chief, Black Moon advised him about his duties. Sitting Bull personally asked Black Moon to conduct the Sun Dance planned in 1876. By acceding to the request, it was Black Moon's privilege to announce that Sitting Bull had been granted a vision in which he saw cavalrymen toppling off their horses with their heads down and their hats falling off; a voice was heard saying, "I give you these because they have no ears." The vision was interpreted as a prophesy of victory in a forthcoming encounter. The validity of the prediction was confirmed that same year on the Little Big Horn River in Montana when the Sioux and their allies triumphed over General George Custer and his cavalry units.

Jumping Bull. ? to 1858.

Prior to his mystic experience, he was known to Hunkpapa Sioux tribesmen as Returns Again. His special gift was to understand and communicate with animals. While sitting by a campfire with friends one evening, the group espied a lone bull nearby; it stood still and repeatedly uttered strange sounds. Listening attentively, Returns Again interpreted them and realized that he was being offered new names to keep for himself or to bestow on others. The names were Sitting Bull, Jumping Bull, Bull Standing With Cow and Lone Bull. This was a very sacred gift, for the names were associated with the four divisions of life: Infancy, Youth, Maturity and Old Age. He immediately chose Sitting Bull for his new name.

In 1848, he honored his only son, Slow, who performed a very brave deed at the age of fourteen, by giving him the name Sitting Bull. He took for himself the name Jumping Bull (Tatanka Psica). Upon his death in 1858, Jumping Bull was buried at Cedar Creek near Lemmon, South Dakota.

Sitting Bull. 1834 to 1890.

He was named Hunkesni (Slow), not because he lacked agility and vitality, but because from infancy, he was thoughtful and deliberate—cautious rather than abrupt. But as he grew in strength and knowledge, Sitting Bull, born in 1834 at Grand River, South Dakota, thrilled to fearless exploits as a Hunkpapa youth and was placed in the care of his uncle, Four Horns. It was from him that Sitting Bull learned the art of oratory.

To commemorate a brave act during adolescence, he was given the name Tatanka Iyatake (Sitting Buffalo Bull). In later years, when his medium height framed a sturdy, compact body, he still reveled in humorous accounts of his experiences. Around the age of twenty-two, Sitting Bull was permanently lamed in one foot by a bulletwound. He belonged to the New Dog and Strong Hearts Societies, and became a skilled medicine man.

When General Custer attacked Sitting Bull's camp on the Little Big Horn in Montana in 1876, the Hunkpapa chief raced his war horse Blackie to the top of a hill, gaining an advantageous view of the entire battlefield. Using his lance decorated with long streamers, Sitting Bull gave silent commands to warrior groups engaged in the defensive action. Before the day ended, Custer and most of his men lay dead, and the victory foretold in Sitting Bull's vision became a reality.

Fearing white vengeance for Custer's death, Sitting Bull led his band, including his wife and twin sons, toward the "medicine line" (Canadian border) which they reached in 1877, encamping at Wood Mountain. By 1881, the people were near death from starvation because the buffalo had been slaughtered by whites and Canada refused their requests for food and a permanent reserve. The several women among his chiefs replaced warriors killed by U.S. forces, leaving the band's defense ranks dangerously depleted.

Sitting Bull returned to the U.S. and was imprisoned for two years. After his release, he lived on the Standing Rock Reservation. In 1885, he became the star attraction of the William (Buffalo Bill) Cody Wild West Show. The Chief was a heroic figure whose influence Federal authorities feared. He was killed by an Indian police force detailed to arrest him.

Sitting Bull's death in 1890 was announced to the Sioux by a single rider on horseback, poised on the crest of a hill in the early light of dawn, singing the fallen warrior's death song. When the song ended, the lone rider called out the mournful words, "Sitting Bull is no more."

He was buried at Ft. Yates Standing Rock Agency in North Dakota. But in 1953, his body was exhumed for reburial on a hilltop overlooking the Missouri River Valley in the vicinity of Mobridge, South Dakota; a granite shaft marks the site.

Sitting Bull had several wives and many children. One who survived him was an adopted son, John Sitting Bull, a deaf-mute who communicated in sign language.

Lakota

Adage. *See* Apache, proverb.

Dallas Chief Eagle. 1925 to ?

Activism in defense of native American rights did not end with the deaths of historic native American heroes. Dallas Chief Eagle was their modern counterpart. He was born in 1925 on the Rosebud Reservation in South Dakota, a descendant of Crazy Horse with whom he was often compared.

The U.S. Marine Corps veteran attended the University of Idaho at Pocatello, Tulsa City College, and Oklahoma A & M.

Chief Eagle was a humorist, lecturer, artist and author. His book, *Winter Count,* from which the statements of Blue Thunder, Chiefeagle and Turtleheart are quoted, is a metaphorical account of native American history immediately preceding the death of Crazy Horse in 1877. He applied his knowledge of public and industrial relations to increase the tribe's economy through tourism on reservations.

In 1967, the Teton Sioux elected him their chief. He was the first to hold this title since 1868, when it was bestowed on Red Cloud, whose pipe Chief Eagle received to mark the occasion. The Lakota chief died prematurely in the latter 1970s.

John Fire/Lame Deer. 1903 to 1979.

A log cabin near Pine Ridge and Rosebud reservations in South Dakota was the site of Lame Deer's birth in 1903. Missionaries named his father Silas and the reservation agent added the surname "Fire," but among the people, he was known as Wawi Yohi Ya (Let Them Have Enough). His mother, Sally Red Blanket, was a woman of great beauty. Lame Deer's paternal grandfather was Cante Witko (Crazy Heart), the son of Chief Tahca Ushte. Good Fox, who survived the Wounded Knee Creek Massacre but died in 1928, and Pte Sa Ota Win (Plenty White Buffalo) were his maternal grandparents.

Lame Deer was a wicasa wakan (holy man) of the Lakota, an author, humorist and articulate observer of life, both past and present. His legal name was John Fire, but he used still another, Alice Jitterbug, a character-name he developed for a fairgrounds act. He preferred to be called Lame Deer, the name of his paternal great-grandfather, Chief Tahca Ushte (Lame Deer), leader of the Miniconjou.

A medicine man told Lame Deer of a vision which revealed that Crazy Horse, an ally of Tahca Ushte, would return as a Black man. Coincidentally, inhabitants of Oyotunji in Beaufort County, South Carolina, live in the style of their forefathers. The community was established in 1969 by a group of Blacks who have denounced white culture and twentieth century ways. Lame Deer received eagle-and-owl medicine during a vision occurring shortly after his mother's death in 1920.

In 1941, Lame Deer was inducted by the United States Army and served overseas. He was conductor of Sun Dance ceremonies for several years and teacher to young tribesmen showing the aptitude and desire to become medicine men. He lived in Winner, South Dakota, with his wife, Ida, before his death in 1979.

Proverb. *See* Apache, proverb.

Luther Standing Bear. 1868 to ?
Luther Standing Bear's boyhood name was Ota Kte (Plenty Kill). He was the first son of Chief Standing Bear (Mato Najin') and Pretty Face. The family lived near Beaver Creek in the Wamblee District of Pine Ridge Reservation in South Dakota. Luther's sister, Her Black Blanket, was the wife of Crazy Horse. When he was about ten years old, Luther acted as a scout for the cavalry. At age eleven, he was among the first to enter Carlisle Indian School in Pennsylvania.

Luther learned to play the bugle and was invited to join the school band. He also became proficient on the cornet and played both instruments during concerts in New York City and Philadelphia. On one visit to New York City, the band was asked to participate in dedication ceremonies; Luther led the band as it played and marched across the Brooklyn Bridge for its inaugural opening. He was trained in tinsmithing but he continued his education with a minister on the reservation and was hired to teach in the Rosebud Agency School.

In 1898, he was employed as an interpreter for the William "Buffalo Bill" Cody Wild West Show. During a tour in 1903, he was accompanied by his wife Nellie de Cory; their daughter was born in Birmingham, England, when Alexandra was Queen. To memorialize the event, the infant was named Alexandra Birmingham Cody Standing Bear—Cody was her godfather.

On the New York City stage, he performed in *The Race of Man*. He also lectured and began to write books after his contract ended with Cody. In 1905, before an audience of over sixteen thousand gathered to celebrate the annual Fourth of July Sun Dance, Luther was installed as a chief.

He moved to Hollywood, California, in 1912 to perform in motion pictures. By 1927, he operated his own employment agency serving native American clients, and completed a book about his father and remembrances of life among his people.

Mdewakanton Sioux

Wabashaw. 1825 to 1876.

Wabashaw was born around 1825 to an Ojibwa captive near Winona, Minnesota. He was the third in a succession of chiefs named Wabashaw when he assumed leadership of the Kiyuksa Band in 1836. The name has been rendered as Wapasha, Wapahasha, and Wabasha; it is thought to derive from the Sioux words *wapa* (leaf) and *sha* (red). Also known as Joseph, he was diminutively proportioned and had a benevolent disposition. His camp below Lake Pepin was one of many Mdewakanton villages thriving along the Mississippi River.

Equipment used by whites intrigued Wabashaw; he realized that these could benefit his people and became a friendly, willing advocate of white culture. However, his genuine admiration for Euro-Americans did not preclude being cautious about relying on their promises.

The dominant society's politics created boundless confusion for native Americans. By the time Minnesota had become a state in 1858, the flags of France, England, Spain, the Colony of Virginia, the Northwest Territory, and the territories of Louisiana, Indiana, Illinois, Michigan, Missouri, Iowa, and Wisconsin had flown over portions or, in some cases, all of the land comprising the state. Most native American titles to land in Minnesota Territory were extinguished by 1851. Wabashaw's band was removed to a reservation on the Upper Iowa River in Iowa during 1862. Later, they were moved to the Niobrara Reservation in Nebraska, where Wabashaw died in 1876. His son, Napoleon, succeeded him as chief.

In the capitol area of St. Paul, Minnesota, Wabasha Street defines a grand concourse dominated by the thirty-six-foot-high onyx statue of the "Indian God of Peace."

Oglala Sioux

Black Elk. 1862 to 1950.

Black Elk was the fourth in his family to bear this illustrious name. He was born in 1862 when his parents, Sees The White Cow and Hehaka Sapa (Black Elk), were camped along the Little

Powder River which courses through Wyoming and Montana.

A man of intense spiritual devotion, Black Elk's first mystical experience occurred when he was five years old. However, he had another vision at age nine which had a lifelong effect on him because it revealed the tribe's future and his role as a holy man. Attaining his goal of a personal religious enlightenment, Black Elk dramatized it in the Horse Dance.

In 1887, Black Elk toured Europe with the William "Buffalo Bill" Cody Wild West Show. He was chosen to perform before Queen Victoria because of his knowledge of and skill in enacting traditional dances. Illness forced him to withdraw from the Cody show. He stayed in France to recuperate, and afterwards joined the Mexican Joe Show, appearing in Germany and France. But he was discomforted by a vision he had during his recent illness which disclosed the terrible plight of the Sioux, and he returned home.

Black Elk lived his final years on the Pine Ridge Reservation in South Dakota. It always grieved him to recall the disastrous fate of Indian nations and the downfall of their culture which swept him from a youth of freedom to an old age in confinement. The Oglala holy man died in 1950 at Manderson, South Dakota.

He had two sons, Nick whose mother was Kate Bissonette, and Ben whose mother was Angelina Bissonette. Ben Black Elk is a teacher and university lecturer; he was often photographed by visitors to the Mt. Rushmore Memorial in South Dakota.

Buffalo Ceremony Conductor. Ancient.

Among the Oglala Sioux, it was customary for pubescent females to begin assuming greater responsibility in the home. To obtain for her the blessings and protection of Buffalo Spirit, a girl's parents could request the performance of a Buffalo Ceremony.

This was a private rite for a specific individual. His assistance was sought for the young woman because Buffalo Spirit was the guardian of industry, chastity, hospitality, and fertility. The ritual is a solemn plea for his protection against Iktomi who makes women foolish; Anog Ite, the deceitful spirit who provokes women to do shameful things; Hohnogica, who often stirred up trouble for women who became mothers; and Wazi the Wizard, who might nullify any undertaking. The ceremony leader further admonished the woman to display generosity, integrity, and fortitude.

Crazy Horse. 1849 to 1877.

Crazy Horse was born around 1849 near Rapid Creek, South Dakota. In youth and manhood, he was slender and small-boned; his somewhat light complexion, burned dark by the hot Plains sun, lent a vague shade of contrast to his brown curly hair. Boyhood friends called him Curly and Light-Haired Boy; in later years he was also called His Horse Is Looking, and Quiet Man. His historically famous name derived from his father, Tasunca Witco, an Oglala holy man; literally, it means "his horse is crazy." Chiefs Red Cloud and Spotted Tail were his uncles; Black Elk and Flying Hawk were his cousins.

In his youth, he was accorded the tribe's most coveted honor when nominated to the Scalp Shirt Society whose duty it was to keep intruders from the camp. At seventeen, Crazy Horse joined Red Cloud's campaign against the construction of forts along the Bozeman Trail.

A mutual attraction developed between Crazy Horse and Black Buffalo, a married woman who came to live with him. But her husband, No Water, refusing to grant her the customary woman's right to leave her husband at will, shot the Oglala brave in the face, permanently scarring his chin and jaw. Crazy Horse was prevailed upon to return the woman to her husband; in subsequent years, he had several wives.

Oppressed by personal adversities and the tribe's mounting problems with Federal regulators, Crazy Horse sought relief and guidance in solitary meditation. Black Elk said of him, "Our great chief and priest Crazy Horse obtained most of his greatness and power by regular fasting and lamenting for a vision; he did this on many occasions throughout the year. He was blessed with visions of the Shadow, a prancing horse, the Rock, the Badger, the Day, and the Spotted Eagle. Through these he received both holiness and power." Although he participated in almost every major Sioux campaign against the U.S. Army during the late 1800s, Crazy Horse was never wounded or captured in the field.

In battle, he was the man of his visions: his face was marked with red and black paint designed to conceal his scarred chin and jaw; white hailstone spots dotted his cheeks. Riding before his band of Sioux and Cheyenne warriors, he urged them on with his favorite war cry, "Today is a good day to die."

When other bands fled to Canada in 1876, Crazy Horse remained near the Black Hills. But his camps were continuously destroyed by cavalry units, leaving the people destitute and starving. Without rest, food and time to store-up provisions, continued resistance to punitive military expeditions seemed counter-productive. Crazy Horse and the one thousand one hundred people under his leadership arrived at the Red Cloud Agency in Nebraska in May 1877.

The stable, quiet life he yearned for eluded him. None of his actions could be suspect of inciting the people to revolt, yet white men were wary of the charismatic leader and harassed him at every opportunity. Crazy Horse went to Ft. Robinson in Nebraska to confer with the post commander about the annoyances. On arrival, he was placed in military custody. Abhorring the idea of incarceration and the injustice of his arrest, the Oglala warrior resisted and was mortally bayoneted by one of the soldiers. Crazy Horse died on September 5, 1877. His parents buried him in a place never revealed to a white person; the grave is thought to be near Porcupine Creek. There were many contrasts in the landscape of this man's life. Crazy Horse was a man of solitary habit, humble and devoted to prayer, yet he was also the fearless leader of vast numbers of men whose daily lives were touched by an alien terror.

In 1979, like an echo more than a century old, Dave Long, grandson of Crazy Horse, proclaimed that the religiously-and-culturally significant Black Hills are not for sale. He and other Sioux have rejected a court-awarded settlement which would pass title to the land to the Federal Government.

Flying Hawk. 1852 to 1931.

Flying Hawk was the son of Chief Black Fox and Iron Cedarwoman, an Oglala. He was born in 1852 near Rapid City, South Dakota. Elected chief at age thirty-two, his courage and foresightedness were frequently tested during white penetration of the Western frontier. He sorrowed over the starvation, sickness, and social disruption that followed in the trail of pioneer settlers and transient prospectors. Knowing that his decisions affected both present and future generations, he sought seclusion to meditate and pray.

Flying Hawk's uncle, Sitting Bull, gave him a peace pipe which had been used to consumate many important treaties. He retained possession of it for fifty years, relinquishing it shortly before his death in 1931. The ceremonial pipe was thought to be over one hundred years old at the time.

Flying Hawk performed in the William "Buffalo Bill" Cody Wild West Show, the Colonel Miller 101 Ranch Show and the Sells-Floto Show. Husky and vigorous into old age, Flying Hawk included dancing, buffalo chasing, and rough-riding in his act when he was seventy-six years old. He retired to a cabin in the Badlands.

In 1929, Flying Hawk dictated his impressions of events in North American history for publication. He died two years later at Pine Ridge, South Dakota.

He Dog. Flourished 1800s.

Sunka Bloka (He Dog) was subchief of a mixed Oglala and Miniconjou band consisting of about fourteen lodges. Red Cloud was his uncle; Crazy Horse was a friend and a fellow-member of the Scalp Shirt Society. Traditionally, He Dog's family were tribal historians. His nephew, Amos Bad Heart Bull, was a well-known illustrator of Oglala history.

In 1876, He Dog and his band were visiting Cheyenne Chief Two Moons at Little Powder River in Montana when Colonel J. J. Reynolds ordered a surprise attack on the camp. The cavalry troops were successfully repulsed and consequently, Colonel Reynolds was court-marshalled for his failure.

He Dog represented Pine Ridge Reservation, South Dakota, at a conference in Washington, D.C., during which important changes in the administration of Sioux affairs were agreed to. One provision stipulated that military officers rather than political patronage appointees would serve as agents on the reservations.

He Dog had always been kind and thoughtful of others. His consideration was returned in the tender care given to him by those on whom he depended as increasing blindness darkened his world. Neither time nor nature dimmed his memories; even at the age of ninety-two, he longed for the old lifestyle.

He was honored with the naming of He Dog School on Cut Meat Creek, present-day Parmalee, South Dakota. Years later, a new brick school was built on the Rosebud Reservation and also named for him.

Village elder.
By their ability to survive the rigors of a long life, the elderly proved the superiority of their medicine and spiritual power. Young people were eager to learn the secrets of aged tribesmen and listened carefully whenever they had something to say. Old people were admired, honored as wise men and women, and dearly loved for the stories they told.

Morals, social precepts, and spiritual guidelines were taught by the elderly. Their story lessons told about the tribe's culture heroes, the Medicine Wheel, and the ever-popular Trickster whose antics made the lodges resound with laughter. The Trickster figure, far from being ideal, existed as a model of the average person to provide seemingly endless tales which made education a joy for both the young and their elderly teachers.

Young Man Afraid Of His Horse. 1830 to 1900.
Only men with the qualities of excellence were honored with the name Man Afraid Of His Horse (Tasunk Kokipapi). It notified all who heard it that he was so courageous and feared by his enemies that although he was not in view, the sight of his horse alone drove them away in awed intimidation.

Young Man Afraid Of His Horse belonged to the Elk Scraper and Scalp Shirt Societies. He was a contemporary of Dull Knife and Crazy Horse, sharing with them the drama of heroic strife in a perilous pursuit of freedom. In 1865, he participated in a charge on the Platte River Bridge, an important assault against troops at Ft. Phil Kearny, Nebraska. Battles increased in frequency and intensity as white settlers moved westward; conflicts plagued both races until a compromise was reached in 1868 at Ft. Laramie, Wyoming. Young Man Afraid Of His Horse ceased warring against the dominant society, but he never waivered in his determination to limit cession of tribal property to the 1868 treaty terms. However, he did attend several conferences in Washington, D.C., to sort out the tangled relationship between native Americans and Euro-Americans.

There were men of good intent on both sides pitifully unable
to prevail against historic patterns of subjugation, lust for gold,
religious fanatacism, and the iron-willed discipline that characterizes men impelled by grandiose schemes.

Young Man Afraid Of His Horse recognized the injustice
of Federal policies toward native Americans, but labored hard
to convince tribesmen of peaceful coexistence as a means of
survival. The Oglala war chief died in 1900 on the Pine Ridge
Reservation in South Dakota when he was seventy years old.

Plains Sioux

Proverb. *See* Apache, proverb.

Santee Sioux

Chased-by-Bears. 1843 to ?

Mato Kuwapi (Chased-by-Bears), a Santee Sioux, was born
in 1843. He reached manhood during a period notable for
encounters between native Americans, the United States Government, and western pioneers. The nation's history of that time was
also his own. In 1890, after the death of Sitting Bull and the
Wounded Knee Creek Massacre, a somber quiet enveiled the
people, and they withdrew to reservations to grieve for their dead.

In 1918, the Bureau of American Ethnology published
Chased-by-Bears' interpretation of the Sun Dance; it is a deeply
devout expression of the meaning, sacredness, and spirit of the
ceremony. The most important celebration among Plains Indians,
the Sun Dance reemphasizes virtues taught throughout the year.
To complete the days-long rite requires characteristics highly
esteemed by native Americans—generosity, integrity, courage,
and fortitude. It is a time when the people turn their thoughts
to brotherhood and a healing of the tribal soul. Its origin, like
those of other religious rites, lies in the faith and hope common
to all humanity.

Ohiyesa. 1858 to 1939.

In the white man's world, he was known as Charles A.
Eastman, medical doctor, author, lecturer. He was born in 1858

near Redwood Falls, Minnesota, but from around 1862 until 1873, he lived with his uncle, Mysterious Medicine, among the Santee Sioux in British Columbia. He was still a toddler when his mother Mary, daughter of Captain Seth Eastman of the United States Army, became ill and died. His father, Many Lightnings, was away at that time so the child was placed in the care of his paternal grandmother. Uncheedah (Grandmother) and Mysterious Medicine named him Hakadah (The Pitiful Last). He was rewarded with a new name, Ohiyesa (The Winner), after his play gained crucial points for his victorious lacrosse team. Ohiyesa returned to the U.S. for his education, entering Dartmouth College, Hanover, New Hampshire, in 1883. After Dartmouth, he enrolled in the Boston University medical school, graduating in 1890.

Dr. Eastman was appointed to the Crow Creek and Pine Ridge medical facilities in South Dakota. During his first winter there in 1890, Pine Ridge Agency was locked in by a blizzard, but news of native Americans having been massacred by U.S. troops filtered in. Three days later, the storm abated and Dr. Eastman led seventy-five Lakota to the scene at Wounded Knee Creek. His heritage and training as a physician dedicated to the perpetuation of human life combined in overwhelming sorrow at the sight of frozen bodies of men, women and children, being thrown into a common grave while cavalrymen encircled the area with rifles pointed at the mourners. Miraculously, there were a few survivors, and Eastman attended to their medical needs.

After holding several government positions related to Indian affairs, Dr. Eastman entered private practice in St. Paul, Minnesota. In 1911, he addressed the Universal Congress of Races in London. He authored several books and appeared on behalf of native Americans before Congress and in the judicial system. In 1927, he lectured at Oxford, Cambridge and Liverpool Universities, at Eton College, and other schools in England. Eastman's extensive speaking engagements brought him international fame.

Dr. Eastman's wife, Elaine Goodale, with whom he had six children, gained prominence in her own right as a poet. Dr. Eastman was living in Detroit, Michigan, at the time of his death in 1939.

Uncheedah. Flourished 1800s.

In the Siouan language, "uncheedah" means grandmother. Strong-willed, self-assured, independent, and intelligent are words that best describe this daughter of a chief of the "Dwellers Among The Leaves." Nothing was too inconsequential to deserve her keen observation and evaluation; the knowledge thus gained was retained, then quickly retrieved whenever it could be most beneficially applied. As a medicine woman, Uncheedah's moral behaviour had to be extraordinary, for it was understood that only the good and wise were blessed and guided by the Great Mystery from whom such talents flowed.

Women of the tribe relied on Uncheedah not only for medical advice, but also for personal leadership. Her reputation for courage derived from occasions when her fast response and alertness saved the camp from destruction when invaded during the men's absence.

During the late 1850s, the native American soul lay exposed and wounded, tormented by death and upheaval as the white man pursued his "Manifest Destiny." Uncheedah's son, Many Lightnings, was missing and presumed dead; his wife lay dying, leaving their infant son in the care of her kindly mother-in-law. Though the grief was deep and painful, greater yet was the grandmother's love for her grandson, so she willingly assumed responsibility for him.

Because of the circumstances of his childhood, her beloved grandson was named Hakadah (The Pitiful Last), the only name by which Uncheedah ever addressed him, even after he had become renowned in North America and Europe as Dr. Charles A. Eastman.

During her many years of widowhood, Uncheedah managed to support herself and maintain a home in Minnesota. At age eighty-two, her energy and tenacity were undiminished. She could still walk twenty-five miles without rest and without signs of fatigue; in addition to her customary chores, she also built canoes.

Teton Sioux

Blue Thunder. *See* Lakota, Dallas Chief Eagle.

Chiefeagle. *See* Lakota, Dallas Chief Eagle.

Proverb. *See* Apache, proverb.

Turtleheart. *See* Lakota, Dallas Chief Eagle.

Vision quest prayer. *See* Crow, voice in a vision quest.

White Buffalo Calf Woman. Ancient.

The albino buffalo, as a perceptible manifestation of the animating forces of the universe, is frequently found in legends of the Plains tribes. Its coming portends a momentous change in the lives of the people and accompanies the presentation of a beneficial cultural gift.

The first appearance of White Buffalo Calf Woman is traditionally set in the tenth century; she is credited with establishing essential customs which are commemorated in the Feast of the Buffalo on the third day of the Sun Dance. At that time, it is said, the Sioux Nation was gathered for its annual assembly, but buffalos were scarce and the people were hungry. The tribe was saved from starvation when White Buffalo Calf Woman brought them gifts of maize and the Sacred Pipe.

She is depicted as a woman of exquisite beauty who called herself an emissary of the Buffalo tribe and a messenger of Wakonda, whose blessings she carried to the people. The Sacred Pipe, she explained, was to be used as a peacemaker. Like the Christian cross, it symbolizes the spiritual salvation of humanity, and like the Hebrew Ark, it is proof of the sacred covenant between Wakonda and the people.

The original Sacred Pipe is referred to as Ptehincala Huhu Canunpa (Buffalo Calf Bone Pipe). It was given for safekeeping to Chief Standing Hollow Horn to whose Without Bows People Band White Buffalo Calf Woman first appeared. The chief and each successor guardian of the pipe lived for nearly one hundred years.

Yankton Sioux

Chacopee and the Wooden Man. Ancient.

This episode is one of many of its type used to recount the condition of the people in ancient times. The mystical Wooden Man represents the wisdom of the gods and their continuous solicitude for the human race. Chacopee, the youth of prodigious strength, symbolizes the quality of man. It teaches that human life is an ordeal requiring courage and social loyalty, but from these emerge both hope and insights beneficial to mankind.

Reverend Vine Deloria, Sr. Contemporary.

The Reverend Deloria was born to a family of scholars, churchmen, and chiefs. His father, Tipi Sapa, became chief of the White Swan Yanktoni at the age of eighteen. Tipi Sapa anglicized his surname, Des Lauriers, to Deloria and after completing college at Platsmouth, Nebraska, entered the Episcopalian ministry. Known thereafter as The Reverend Philip Deloria, he spent forty years in one of the earliest Christian ministries among the Plains tribes. Reverend Philip Deloria is depicted among the sculpted figures in the work "Christ in Majesty," located in the Episcopal National Cathedral, Washington, D.C.

In 1916, Philip Deloria's son, Vine, left Standing Rock Reservation to attend school. He returned fifteen years later as an ordained minister in the Episcopalian church. Reverend Vine Deloria conducted services appropriate to his native American congregation; hymnals such as *Dakota Odowan* and *Wakan Cekiye Odowan* were used.

His thirty-seven years as a missionary included several responsible positions within the church, including National Council assistant secretary in the Domestic Missions division, the first native American to hold a national executive post in the Episcopalian faith.

Before his retirement from active missionary work, Reverend Deloria was rector of St. Paul's Episcopal Church in Vermillion, South Dakota, and archdeacon of the Niobrara Deaconry during his residency in Pierre, South Dakota.

Tlingit

A mother's counsel. *See* Oglala Sioux, village elder.

Moral tradition. *See* Omaha, moral teaching.

Wanapum

Old One. Flourished early 1700s to early 1800s.

The Wanapum lived and fished at Priest Rapids, Washington, during the late 1700s. But advancing age and the elements forced Old One to pass the time by contemplating the past and bemoaning the future. The sadness of his thoughts etched deep wrinkles upon his leathery face and clouded his already dimly-seeing eyes. A blanket and large fur cap shielded him from the icy winds of winter along the Chiawana (Columbia River) as he chanted songs and told stories to anyone willing to listen with an open mind and heart.

He was a medicine man and teacher of the tribe's creation legends. Old One told of how eons ago Nami Piap destroyed the world, once by fire, and again when he made the waters rise to flood the land; and of the time when Nami Piap loosened the earth to crush and abolish those who were forgetful and failed to live in the way that pleased him. Old One recalled the time of the Ancient Ones, those whom Nami Piap created in the beginning, and who lived in a land of happiness where evil was unknown and the people never worked or hungered. The Sacred Island was the place where Nami Piap provided for all their needs.

When Old One died, he was wrapped in buckskin and laid in the longhouse while the people chanted ancient songs in a last farewell. They carried Old One to a mountain top to bury him in the earth he loved; his body was placed beneath a canoe, then both were sealed under rocks. Afterwards Old One's house was set on fire according to custom while the people sang songs of lamentation.

Although Old One was gone, his teachings found fertile soil and took root in the slowly nurtured wisdom of his pupil, the child Smowhala, who would someday establish a new religion.

Smowhala. 1820 to 1908.

Born around 1820 at Wallula in Priest Rapids, Washington, Smowhala (The Prophet) was destined to become an influential religious leader. He was a congenital hunchback whose renown originated in his skill as a medicine man. When Smowhala was about forty years old, he and a rival shaman came to physical blows over a disagreement. Smowhala was severely injured and left for dead.

But Smowhala recovered to begin an odyssey to the Pacific Coast as far as Mexico and North through Arizona, Utah, and Nevada. After his return to the Columbia River region, he often withdrew into a visionary trance or dream state. In one vision, he received a set of precepts and symbols to use as the basis for a new religion. Through persuasive oratory and an attitude of sincerity, Smowhala gained many adherents who were called Dreamers because they aspired to a self-induced trance. The Dreamers were first heard of around 1870. The religion was a source of inspiration to people of many tribes; in essence, it gave voice to their yearning for a past lifestyle, before the white man came.

During ceremonies, Smowhala wore a shirt depicting symbols of the Dreamer religion—the sacred colors white, red, and yellow; the sun, moon, and a star. He explained that the sun represented life; the moon and the star were the drumbeat—the pulse of the universe. The color of the sun was white and stood for one day of life. The yellow moon was one month of life. The seven-pointed star was red and represented one week of life. These meanings had been given in ancient times, and therefore, the symbolism had a long history of acceptance by the people.

The most sacred ceremonial object was the Wowshuxkluh, a bird carved by Smowhala from the type of wood on which the original bird had perched in his dream. As proof of its appearance, it—an oriole whose Indian name means "Knocking Off Berries With A Piece Of Stick"—left some feathers on the tree limb; Smowhala attached these to the carving to form its tail.

After Smowhala's death around 1908, the Dreamer rituals were continued by his son Yóyouni who was also called Little Smowhala. Yóyouni was succeeded by Smowhala's nephew, Puckhyahtoot (The Last Prophet).

Winnebago

Sam Blow Snake. Flourished 1900s.

At his birth in the latter half of the nineteenth century, the name Hágaga was chosen for him by his grandmother. Hers was the last family of pure Winnebago ancestry and the name memorialized her descent. Members of the powerful Thunderbird Clan, Sam Blow Snake's parents, Charles Blow Snake and Lucy Goodvillage, were prominent among the Winnebago and in tribal politics.

Renowned as a fisherman and hunter, it was his father's custom to invite all of the people to a feast after a successful hunt for game on the Mississippi near LaCrosse, Wisconsin, or a spear-fishing expedition for sturgeon at Black River Falls. On such occasions, he related the tribe's history and encouraged his family to honor ancient ceremonies. Accordingly, Sam Blow Snake's excellent bass voice was often heard on the reservation during his participation in the Brave Dance and Medicine Dance. His brother-in-law, Thunder Cloud, a man of exceptional powers, was unique among the Winnebago in claiming that he was living his third life on Earth as the reincarnation of the culture hero Hare.

Sam Blow Snake became a professional singer and dancer. At the end of the performing season, he donned "citizen's clothing" and was employed as a log-roller. At the age of twenty-three, he counted his first coup and celebrated the event with a new name—Big Winnebago. Over six feet tall and muscular, the name was descriptively appropriate.

He was conscientious, persevering, enterprising, and ambitious to succeed. However, Sam Blow Snake's frequent moves between the reservation and white community caused deeply disturbing, ambivalent anxieties about his position within the two cultures. His search for a satisfactory solution ultimately involved him in a peyote-centered religion. Gradually, he found in it the contentment which had eluded him in the past. His handwritten autobiography in the Winnebago language was translated and published during this period in 1920.

This Newly Created World. Ancient.

The author of this composition is unknown, but the portent of its phrases fascinated those who heard it and repeated it; thus, it has been preserved. Songs of visions were concise summaries using key words to evoke the vision's theme, tone, mood, and content. These sketches were full of imagery that recalled the entirety of the vision.

During tense encounters with enemies, when breastworks were erected and decoy tactics employed, criers moving behind the line of warriors shouted out orders. Beyond them, women would gather to sing "strong heart songs" and urge the men to victory.

Through song, the native American appealed to the ubiquitous unseen power for help in search of food and for success in the healing power of the herbs he gathered. In song, he found an expression of pleasure in his happiness, and comfort when his road was difficult. Songs preserved his tribal history, customs, and ceremonies.

Song, with or without words, was intrinsic to the existence of the native American; a man without a song was a poor man.

Yaqui

Rosalio Moisés. 1896 to 1969.

His legal name was Rosalio Valenzuela Hurtado, but in childhood he was familiarly called Rosa Lingo or Lio. Rosalio was born in 1896, in Mexico, where his father mined ore on the Colorada Mines. Political strife made life tenuous for the people and many left the country. Rosalio was nine when his family moved to Arizona where his father established a prominent position among the Sierra Yaqui.

In public schools, Rosalio learned to speak English as fluently as he spoke Spanish and Yaqui. The original draft of his autobiography was hand-written in English.

Rosalio found work as an interpreter, and when he visited New York City and Boston in 1931, he was able to converse with foreign sailors about their countries. Rosalio spent long hours on the docks, enjoying the sight of ships entering the harbor or lying at berth.

For many years, he lived alone on a farm in Lubbock County, Texas, where he raised cotton and performed odd jobs. He built a Yaqui ramada for the West Texas Museum at Texas Technology College in Lubbock and helped on archaeological field expeditions. After 1953, he lived and worked on a Texas farm during harvest season, but returned to Tucson, Arizona, and Sonoran Yaqui villages each winter.

Rosalio was a *fariseo*, taking part in the carefully perpetuated Easter rites of Holy Week. The stately religious festival is still observed in Pascua, the Yaqui village just outside Tucson. Rosalio Moisés was living in Tucson at the time of his death in 1969.

Zuñi

Advice to a widow. During the first year after her husband's death, a woman observed certain mourning restrictions. According to custom, she scattered prayermeal, passing it four times over her head; she said her prayers silently; she did not eat meat, salt, or grease. No one could touch the widow except her own child. She remained alone and did not participate in camp activities.

When the period of mourning had passed, a male member of her family would come for her, or she was gradually included in the daily affairs of the tribe.

Tribe Unknown

A native American. *See* Eskimo, anonymous.

Anonymous. *See* Eskimo, anonymous.

Anonymous native American. *See* Eskimo, anonymous.

Footnotes

Creation: The Great Circle Is The Universe

1. Paul Radin, *The Road of Life and Death* (New York: Pantheon Books, 1945), p. 254.

2. Joseph E. Brown, *The Sacred Pipe: Black Elk's Account of the Seven Rites of the Oglala Sioux* (Norman: University of Oklahoma Press, 1953), pp. XX, 59.

3. Hyemeyohsts Storm, *Seven Arrows* (New York: Harper & Row Publishers, 1972), p. 21.

4. Charles A. Eastman, *The Soul of the Indian* (Boston: Houghton-Mifflin Co., 1911), pp. 4-6.

5. Frances Densmore, *Nootka and Quileute Music*, Bureau of American Ethnology, bulletin 124 (Washington: Government Printing Office, 1939), p. 285.

6. Marion E. Gridley, *Contemporary American Indian Leaders* (New York: Dodd, Mead & Co., 1972), p. 138.

7. Brown, *op. cit.*, p. 115.

8. Dallas Chief Eagle, *Winter Count* (Colorado Springs: Dentan-Berkeland Printing Co., 1967), p. 210.

9. Polingaysi Qoyawayma, *No Turning Back*, as told to Vada F. Carlson (Albuquerque: University of New Mexico Press, 1964), p. 172.

10. Alice C. Fletcher, Francis LaFlesche, *The Omaha Tribe*, Bureau of American Ethnology, 27th annual report, 1905-1906 (Washington: Government Printing Office, 1911), p. 130.

11. *Ibid.*, pp. 115-116.

12. Charles A. Eastman, *Indian Boyhood* (New York: McClure, Phillips & Co., 1902), p. 21.

13. Luther Standing Bear, *Land of the Spotted Eagle* (Boston: Houghton-Mifflin Co., 1933), p. 14.

14. John Fire/Lame Deer, Richard Erdoes, *Lame Deer, Seeker of Visions* (New York: Simon & Schuster, Touchstone Books, 1972), p. 157.

15. Rosalio Moisés, *A Yaqui Life: The Personal Chronicle of a Yaqui Indian*, with Jane Holden Kelley and William C. Holden (Lincoln: University of Nebraska Press, 1977), p. 92.

16. Frank Waters, *Book of the Hopi* (New York: Ballantine Books, 1969), p. 211.

17. Standing Bear, *Land of the Spotted Eagle, op. cit.*, pp. 201-202.

18. Fletcher, *The Omaha Tribe*, 1911, *op. cit.*, p. 598.

19. Brown, *op. cit.*, p. 31.

20. Mari Sandoz, *Crazy Horse: The Strange Man of the Oglalas* (Lincoln: University of Nebraska Press, 1961), p. 114.

21. Thomas L. McKenney and James Hall, *The Indian Tribes of North America*, 1836, new edition, 3 vols., ed. Frederick Webb Hodge, vol. 1 (Edenburgh: John Grant, 1933), pp. 190-191.

22. Althea Bass, *The Arapaho Way; Memoirs of Carl Sweezy* (New York: Clarkson N. Potter, 1966), p. 68.

23. Chief Eagle, *op. cit.*, p. 210.

24. Brown, *op. cit.*, p. 74.

25. Alice C. Fletcher, *The Hako: A Pawnee Ceremony*, Bureau of American Ethnology, 22nd annual report, part 2, 1900-1901 (Washington: Government Printing Office, 1904), p. 33.

26. Edward Goodbird, *Goodbird the Indian* (New York: Fleming H. Revell Co., 1914), p. 33.

27. Standing Bear, *Land of the Spotted Eagle*, *op. cit.*, p. 50.

28. Brad Steiger, *Medicine Talk* (Garden City, New York: Doubleday & Co., 1975), p. 199.

29. Eastman, *Indian Boyhood*, *op. cit.*, p. 17.

30. Helen Hunt Jackson, *A Century of Dishonor*, 1885, revised (Boston: Little, Brown, & Co., 1909), p. 124.

31. Samuel G. Drake, *The Aboriginal Races of North America*, 15th ed., revised J. W. O'Neill (Phildadelphia: Charles Desilver, 1860), p. 596.

32. Fletcher, *The Hako*, *op. cit.*, p. 107.

33. John Fire/Lame Deer, *op. cit.* p. 46.

34. N. Scott Momaday, *The Way to Rainy Mountain* (Albuquerque: University of New Mexico Press, 1969), p. 83.

35. Fletcher, *The Hako*, *op. cit.*, p. 125.

36. Charles A. Eastman, *The Indian Today* (Garden City, New York: Doubleday, Page & Co., 1915), p. 150.

37. Goodbird, *op. cit.*, pp. 34-35.

38. *The New Haven Register*, 17 October 1976.

39. Standing Bear, *Land of the Spotted Eagle*, *op. cit.*, p. 197.

40. Dolores McAuliffe, ed., *As Long As the Rivers Shall Flow*, calendar, vol. 19 (New York: War Resisters League, 1974), no copyright, n.p.

41. John Fire/Lame Deer, *op. cit.*, p. 79.

42. John G. Neihardt, *Black Elk Speaks* (New York: William Morrow & Co., 1932), pp. 164-165.

43. Goodbird, *op. cit.*, pp. 37-38.

Morality and Law: Links In A Circle Without End

44. Storm, *op. cit.*, p. 163.

45. Click Relander, *Drummers and Dreamers* (Caldwell, Idaho: Caxton Printers, 1956), p. 139.

46. Chief Joseph, "An Indian's Views of Indian Affairs," *North American Review*, vol. CXXVIII, April 1879.

47. Stan Steiner, *The New Indians* (New York: Harper & Row Publishers, 1968), p. 107.

48. Frank B. Linderman, *Plenty-coups, Chief of the Crows* (Lincoln: University of Nebraska Press, 1930, 1957), p. 43.

49. Black Hawk, *Life of Ma-Ka-Tai-Me-She-Kia-Kiak or Black Hawk*, 1833, reprint, *Black Hawk: an autobiography*, ed. Donald Jackson, cloth edition (Urbana: University of Illinois Press, 1955), p. 105.

50. Sun Bear, *Buffalo Hearts* (Spokane, Washington: Bear Tribe Publishing, 1970), p. 28.

51. Edward Ahenakew, *Voices of the Plains Cree*, ed. Ruth M. Bush (Toronto: McClelland & Stewart Limited, 1973), p. 80, reprinted with permission of the Canadian Publishers.

52. Thomas Wildcat Alford, *Civilization*, as told to Florence Drake (Norman: University of Oklahoma Press, 1936), p. 19.

53. Jackson, *A Century of Dishonor*, *op. cit.*, p. 300.

54. Eastman, *The Soul of the Indian*, *op. cit.*, pp. 88-90.

55. Ahenakew, *op. cit.*, p. 69.

56. Ahenakew, *op. cit.*, p. 92.

57. John Fire/Lame Deer, *op. cit.*, p. 208.

58. Sun Bear, *op. cit.*, p. 19.

59. Steiger, *op. cit.*, p. 33.

60. McAuliffe, *op. cit.*, n.p.

61. Frances Densmore, *Teton Sioux Music*, Bureau of American Ethnology, bulletin 61 (Washington: Government Printing Office, 1918), p. 65.

62. Leo W. Simmons, ed., *Sun Chief: The Autobiography of a Hopi Indian* (New Haven: Yale University Press, 1942, 1967), p. 224.

63. Mari Sandoz, *These Were the Sioux* (New York: Hastings House Publishers, 1961), p. 39.

64. Truman Michelson, *The Mythological Origin of the White Buffalo Dance of the Fox Indians*, Bureau of American Ethnology, 40th annual report, 1918-1919, Smithsonian Institution (Washington: Government Printing Office, 1925), p. 69.

65. John Fire/Lame Deer, *op. cit.*, p. 75.

66. Edgar S. Cahn, ed., *Our Brother's Keeper* (Washington: New Community Press, 1969), p. 182.

67. Standing Bear, *Land of the Spotted Eagle*, *op. cit.*, pp. 125-126.

68. Storm, *op. cit.*, p. 161.

69. Drake, *The Aboriginal Races of North America*, *op. cit.*, p. 565.

70. United States, Congress, Senate, *Senate Document #88*, 51st Congress, 1st session, cited in Britton Davis, *The Truth about Geronimo*, second printing, ed. M. M. Quaife (New Haven: Yale University Press, 1963), p. 203.

71. Francis LaFlesche, *The Middle Five*, 1900 (Madison: University of Wisconsin Press, 1963), p. 128.

72. Ahenakew, *op. cit.*, p. 84.

73. Buffalo Child Long Lance, *Long Lance* (New York: Cosmopolitan Book Corp., 1928), p. 38.

74. Grenville Goodwin, *The Social Organization of the Western Apache*, University of Chicago Publications in Anthropology, Ethnology series (Chicago: University of Chicago Press, 1942), p. 258.

75. Jackson, *op. cit.*, p. 299.

76. Fletcher, *The Omaha Tribe*, 1911, *op. cit.*, p. 609 note a.

77. Truman Michelson, *The Singing Around Rite of the Fox Society*, Bureau of American Ethnology, 40th annual report, 1918-1919, Smithsonian Institution (Washington: Government Printing Office, 1925), p. 571.

78. Fletcher, *The Omaha Tribe*, 1911, *op. cit.*, p. 603.

79. Dan Kennedy (Ochankugahe), *Recollections of an Assiniboine Chief*, ed. James R. Stevens (Toronto: McClelland & Stewart Limited, 1972), p. 99, reprinted with permission of the Canadian Publishers.

80. Red Cloud Indian School, Pine Ridge, South Dakota, card, 1975, no copyright, n.p.
81. Qoyawayma, *op. cit.*, p. 71.
82. Paul Radin, *Autobiography of a Winnebago Indian*, University of California Press, Publications in American Archaeology and Ethnology, vol. 16, no. 7, 1920, reprint (New York: Dover Publications, Inc., 1963), p. 73.
83. Fletcher, *The Omaha Tribe*, 1911, *op. cit.*, p. 609 note a.
84. Long Lance, *op. cit.*, p. 149.
85. Ahenakew, *op. cit.*, p. 69.
86. Chief Eagle, *op. cit.*, p. 210.
87. McKenny, *op. cit.*, p. 301.
88. Stanley Vestal, *Sitting Bull, Champion of the Sioux*, 1932, Civilization of the American Indian series #46 (Norman: University of Oklahoma Press, 1957), p. 94.
89. Fletcher, *The Hako: a Pawnee Ceremony*, *op. cit.*, p. 344.
90. Kennedy, *Recollections of an Assiniboine Chief*, *op. cit.*, p. 55.
91. Jackson, *op. cit.*, p. 259.
92. Truman Michelson, *The Way Meskwakie Do When They Die*, Bureau of American Ethnology, 40th annual report, 1918-1919, Smithsonian Institution (Washington: Government Printing Office, 1925), p. 403.
93. McAuliffe, *op. cit.*, n.p.
94. James D. Bemis, *Indian Speeches; delivered by Farmer's Brother and Red Jacket, Two Seneca Chiefs* (Canandaigua, New York: n.n., 1809), n.p.
95. Thomas B. Marquis, *A Warrior Who Fought Custer* (Minneapolis: The Midwest Co., 1931), pp. 364-365.
96. Peter Nabokov, *Two Leggings: the making of a Crow Warrior* (New York: Thomas Y. Crowell Co., 1967), p. 27.
97. Luther Standing Bear, *My People the Sioux* (Boston: Houghton-Mifflin Co., 1928), p. 113.
98. Michelson, *The Singing Around Rite of the Fox Society*, *op. cit.*, p. 555.
99. Alford, *op. cit.*, p. 198.
100. Ahenakew, *op. cit.*, p. 72.
101. Relander, *op. cit.*, p. 24.
102. Storm, *op. cit.*, pp. 163-164.

Wisdom: The Circle Is The Great Medicine Wheel

103. Storm, *op. cit.*, p. 20.
104. Relander, *op. cit.*, p. 143.
105. Eve Ball, *In the Days of Victorio: recollections of a Warm Springs Apache* (Tucson: University of Arizona Press, 1970), p. 11.
106. Fletcher, *The Omaha Tribe*, 1911, *op. cit.*, p. 609 note a.
107. Sun Bear, *op. cit.*, p. 24.
108. Linderman, *Plenty-coups, Chief of the Crows*, *op. cit.*, p. 67.
109. Ahenakew, *op. cit.*, p. 131.
110. Standing Bear, *Land of the Spotted Eagle*, *op. cit.*, p. 159.
111. George Webb, *A Pima Remembers* (Tucson: University of Arizona Press, 1959), p. 89.

112. John Fire/Lame Deer, *op. cit.*, p. 170.
113. Linderman, *Plenty-coups, Chief of the Crows, op. cit.*, p. 71.
114. *Ibid.*, p. 67.
115. Eastman, *Indian Boyhood, op. cit.*, p. 54.
116. Chief Joseph, *op. cit.*, n.p.
117. Peter Freuchen, *Book of the Eskimos* (New York: Fawcett World Library, 1961), p. 154.
118. Linderman, *Plenty-coups, Chief of the Crows, op. cit.*, p. 78.
119. Steiger, *op. cit.*, p. 50.
120. Storm, *op. cit.*, p. 177.
121. Drake, *The Aboriginal Races of North America, op. cit.*, p. 632.
122. Jimalee Burton (Ho-chee-nee), *Indian Heritage, Indian Pride* (Norman: University of Oklahoma Press, 1974), p. 44.
123. Simmons, *op. cit.*, p. 277.
124. Burton, *op. cit.*, p. 136.
125. Qoyawayma, *op. cit.*, p. 55.
126. Eastman, *The Soul of the Indian, op. cit.*, p. 90.
127. Frances Densmore, *The American Indians and Their Music* (New York: The Womans Press, 1926), p. 62.
128. McKenny, *op. cit.*, p. 323.
129. Clyde Kluckhohn and Dorothea Leighton, *The Navaho* (Cambridge, Mass.: Harvard University Press, 1946), p. 226.
130. Chief Eagle, *op. cit.*, p. 38.
131. Michelson, *The Mythological Origin of the White Buffalo Dance of the Fox Indians, op. cit.*, p. 195.
132. Paul Radin, *The Autobiography of a Winnebago Indian*, University of California Publications in American Archaeology and Ethnology, vol. 16, no. 7, part 1, 1919-1920 (Berkeley: University of California Press, 1920), pp. 472-473.
133. Steiger, *op. cit.*, p. 49.
134. Steiner, *op. cit.*, p. 196.
135. Richard S. Brandt, *Hopi Ethics* (Chicago: University of Chicago Press, 1954), p. 128.
136. Michael S. Kennedy, ed., *The Assiniboines, From the Accounts of the Old Ones, Told to First Boy (James Larpenteur Long)*, orig. pub. as *Land of Nakoda, The Assiniboines*, 1942, new edition, Civilization of the American Indian series, no. 58 (Norman: University of Oklahoma Press, 1961), p. lxvii.
137. Vestal, *op. cit.*, p. 9.
138. Standing Bear, *Land of the Spotted Eagle, op. cit.*, p. 160.
139. Alice C. Fletcher and Francis LaFlesche, *The Omaha Tribe*, Bureau of American Ethnology, 27th annual report, 1905-1906, Washington: Government Printing Office, 1911, Bison Book, 2 vols. (Lincoln: University of Nebraska Press, Vol. 2, 1972), p. 331.
140. Leslie Spier, *Yuman Tribes of the Gila River*, University of Chicago Publications in Anthropology, Ethnological series (Chicago: University of Chicago Press, 1933), p. 236.
141. Qoyawayma, *op. cit.*, p. 176.
142. George P. Belden, *Belden, The White Chief; or Twelve Years among the*

Wild Indians of the Plains, ed. General James S. Brisbin (Cincinnati: C. F. Vent, 1870), p. 47.

143. Steiger, *op. cit.,* p. 47.

144. Steiger, *op. cit.,* p. 48.

145. S. M. Barrett, ed., *Geronimo: His Own Story,* 1906 (New York: E. P. Dutton & Co., Inc., 1970), p. 136.

146. Cahn, *op. cit.,* p. 107.

147. St. Ann's Indian Mission, Belcourt, North Dakota, card, 1972, no copyright, n.p.

148. Brandt, *op. cit.,* p. 181.

149. Brandt. *op. cit.,* p. 180.

150. Fletcher, *The Hako: a Pawnee Ceremony, op. cit.,* p. 47.

151. Standing Bear, *Land of the Spotted Eagle, op. cit.,* p. 160.

152. Kennedy, *Recollections of an Assiniboine Chief, op. cit.,* p. 98.

153. Qoyawayma, *op. cit.,* p. 30.

154. Ciyé "Niño" Cochise, *The First Hundred Years of Niño Cochise,* as told to A. Kinney Griffith (New York: Abelard-Schuman, 1971), p. 117.

155. Frank Russell, *The Pima Indians,* Bureau of American Ethnology, 26th annual report, 1904-1905 (Washington: Government Printing Office, 1908), p. 190.

156. Vestal, *op. cit.,* p. 263.

157. Sandoz, *These Were the Sioux, op. cit.,* p. 33.

158. Chief Eagle, *op. cit.,* p. 24.

159. Mentor Williams, ed., *Schoolcraft's Indian Legends* (East Lansing: Michigan State University Press, 1956), p. 275.

160. Belden, *op. cit.,* p. 432.

161. Brandt, *op. cit.,* p. 128.

162. Brandt, *op. cit.,* p. 129.

163. Fletcher, *The Omaha Tribe,* 1911, *op. cit.,* p. 604.

164. Standing Bear, *Land of the Spotted Eagle, op. cit.,* p. 163.

165. Bass, *op. cit.,* p. 15.

166. McAuliffe, *op. cit.,* n.p.

167. Kay Bennett, *Kaibah: Recollections of a Navajo Girlhood* (Los Angeles: Westernlore Press, 1964), p. 27.

168. Fletcher, *The Omaha Tribe,* 1911, *op. cit.,* p. 604.

169. Goodwin, *op. cit.,* p. 688.

170. Alvin M. Josephy, Jr., *The Patriot Chiefs,* 4th edition (New York: Viking Press, 1961), p. 159.

171. Williams, *op. cit.,* p. 222.

172. Brandt, *op. cit.,* p. 128.

173. Fletcher, *The Hako: a Pawnee Ceremony, op. cit.,* p. 172.

Life And Death: The Circle Is Timeless

174. Ethel Brant Monture, *Canadian Portraits: Brant, Crowfoot, Oronhyatkha, Famous Indians* (Toronto: Clarke, Irwin & Co., 1960), p. 120.

175. Washington Matthews, *Navajo Legends,* Memoirs of the Folk-Lore Society, vol. 5 (Boston: Houghton, Mifflin & Co., 1897), p. 69.

176. Linderman, *op. cit.,* p. 144.
177. Relander, *Drummers and Dreamers, op. cit.,* p. 23.
178. Nabokov, *op. cit.,* p. 26.
179. McAuliffe, *op. cit.,* n.p.
180. Qoyawayma, *op. cit.,* p. 179.
181. Michelson, *The Mythological Origin of the White Buffalo Dance of the Fox Indians, op. cit.,* p. 69.
182. Vincent Crapanzano, *The Fifth World of Forster Bennett* (New York: Viking Press, 1972), p. 93.
183. Sandoz, *These Were the Sioux, op. cit.,* p. 39.
184. Fletcher, *The Omaha Tribe,* 1911, *op. cit.,* p. 477.
185. Brown, *op. cit.,* pp. 31-32.
186. Herbert J. Spinden, *Songs of the Tewa* (New York: Exposition of Indian Tribal Arts, 1933), p. 13.
187. Radin, *Autobiography of a Winnebago Indian, op. cit.,* p. 89.
188. John Fire/Lame Deer, *op. cit.,* p. 146.
189. McAuliffe, *op. cit.,* n.p.
190. Fletcher, *The Omaha Tribe,* 1911, *op. cit.,* p. 431.
191. Fletcher, *The Omaha Tribe,* 1911, *op. cit.,* p. 475.
192. Drake, *The Aboriginal Races of North America, op. cit.,* p. 633.
193. Simmons, *op. cit.,* p. 351.
194. John Tebbel and Keith Jennison, *The American Indian Wars* (New York: Harper & Bros., 1960), p. 247.
195. Jackson, *op. cit.,* p. 259.
196. Frances Densmore, *Chippewa Music II,* Smithsonian Institution, Bureau of American Ethnology, bulletin 53 (Washington: Government Printing Office, 1913), p. 157.
197. Ruth Bunzel, *Zuñi Texts,* Publication of the American Ethnological Society, vol. 15 (New York: Stechert, 1933), p. 96.
198. Black Hawk, *Life of Ma-Ka-Tai-Me-She-Kia-Kiak* or *Black Hawk,* 1833, reprint, *Black Hawk: an Autobiography,* ed. Donald Jackson (Urbana: University of Illinois Press, 1964), p. 89.
199. Cochise, *op. cit.,* p. 158.
200. *An Uncommon Controversy,* speech by Chief Seattle delivered in 1855, American Friends Service Committee (Washington: National Congress of American Indians, 1967), p. 29.

The Family: Circles Within Circles

201. Alice Marriott and Carol Rachlin, *American Indian Mythology* (New York: Thomas Y. Crowell Co., 1968), p. 150.
202. Kennedy, *Recollections of an Assiniboine Chief, op. cit.,* p. 81.
203. Vinson Brown, *Voices of Earth and Sky* (Harrisburg, Pennsylvania: Stackpole Books, 1974), p. 86.
204. Sandoz, *These Were the Sioux, op. cit.,* p. 103.
205. Walter Dyk, ed., *Son of Old Man Hat, a Navaho autobiography,* 1938, 1966 (Lincoln: University of Nebraska Press, Bison Book, 1967), pp. 48-49.

206. Brandt, *op. cit.*, p. 260.
207. Fletcher, *The Omaha Tribe*, 1911, *op. cit.*, p. 337.
208. Densmore, *The American Indians and Their Music*, *op. cit.*, p. 85.
209. Kennedy, *The Assiniboines*, *op. cit.*, pp. 28-30.
210. Radin, *Autobiography of a Winnebago Indian*, *op. cit.*, p. 82.
211. Truman Michelson, *How Meskwaki Children Should Be Brought Up*, 1922, in Elsie C. Parsons, ed., *American Indian Life* (New York: The Viking Press, Inc., 1925), p. 84.
212. John R. Swanton, *Tlingit Myths and Texts*, Bureau of American Ethnology, bulletin 39 (Washington: Government Printing Office, 1909), p. 92.
213. Sandoz, *These Were the Sioux*, *op. cit.*, p. 80.
214. Spier, *Yuman Tribes of the Gila River*, *op. cit.*, p. 359.
215. Webb, *op. cit.*, p. 88.
216. Morris E. Opler, *Childhood and Youth in Jicarilla Apache Society*, publication of the Frederick Webb Hodge Anniversary Publication Fund, vol. 5 (Los Angeles: Southwest Museum, 1946), p. 61.
217. Kluckhohn, *op. cit.*, p. 221.
218. Storm, *op. cit.*, p. 14.
219. Black Hawk, 1955, *op. cit.*, p. 103.
220. Ahenakew, *op. cit.*, p. 66.
221. Morris E. Opler, *Apache Odyssey: A Journey Between Two Worlds* (New York: Holt, Rinehart & Winston, 1969), p. 66.
222. Densmore, *Teton Sioux Music*, *op. cit.*, p. 161.
223. Kennedy, *The Assiniboines*, *op. cit.*, p. 60.
224. Standing Bear, *Land of the Spotted Eagle*, *op. cit.*, pp. 69-70.
225. Goodwin, *op. cit.*, p. 453.
226. Brandt. *op. cit.*, pp. 78, 79.
227. Verne F. Ray, *Primitive Pragmatists: the Modoc Indians of Northern California*, ed. Viola E. Garfield, American Ethnological Society, Monograph 38 (Seattle: University of Washington Press, 1963), p. 111.
228. Ahenakew, *op. cit.*, p. 133.
229. Clellan S. Ford, *Smoke From Their Fires*, Institute of Human Relations (New Haven: Yale University Press, 1941), p. 77.
230. Sandoz, *These Were the Sioux*, *op. cit.*, p. 43.
231. Swanton, *Tlingit Myths and Texts*, *op. cit.*, p. 108.
232. Dyk, *Son of Old Man Hat*, *op. cit.*, pp. 70, 71.
233. Kennedy, *The Assiniboines*, *op. cit.*, p. 41.
234. Qoyawayma, *op. cit.*, p. 35.
235. Goodwin, *op. cit.*, p. 312.
236. Michelson, *How Meskwaki Children Should Be Brought Up*, *op. cit.*, p. 86.
237. Opler, *Childhood and Youth in Jicarilla Apache Society*, *op. cit.*, p. 92.
238. Sandoz, *These Were the Sioux*, *op. cit.*, p. 69.
239. J. R. Walker, *The Sun Dance and other Ceremonials of the Teton Dakota*, Anthropology Papers of the American Museum of Natural History, vol. 16, part 2 (New York: American Museum of Natural History, 1917), p. 147.
240. Densmore, *Teton Sioux Music*, *op. cit.*, p. 66.
241. Russell, *op. cit.*, p. 191.

242. Opler, *Apache Odyssey, op. cit.,* p. 250.
243. Radin, *The Autobiography of a Winnebago Indian, op. cit.,* p. 463.
244. Walter Dyk, *Old Mexican: a Navajo Autobiography,* Viking Fund Publications in Anthropology, no. 8 (New York: Viking Fund, 1947), p. 140.
245. Densmore, *The American Indians and Their Music, op. cit.,* p. 15.
246. Sandoz, *These Were the Sioux, op. cit.,* p. 99.
247. Sandoz, *These Were the Sioux, op. cit.,* p. 101.
248. Truman Michelson, *The Autobiography of a Fox Indian Woman,* Bureau of American Ethnology, 40th annual report, 1918-1919, Smithsonian Institution (Washington: Government Printing Office, 1925), p. 299.
249. Long Lance, *op. cit.,* pp. 34-35.
250. Steiger, *op. cit.,* p. 80.
251. Storm, *op. cit.,* p. 120.
252. Alford, *op. cit.,* p. 20.
253. Michelson, *How Meskwaki Children Should Be Brought Up, op. cit.,* p. 83.
254. Kennedy, *Recollections of an Assiniboine Chief, op. cit.,* p. 107.
255. Standing Bear, *My People the Sioux, op. cit.,* p. 112.
256. Fletcher, *The Hako: a Pawnee Ceremony, op. cit.,* p. 365.

The Tribe: The Circle Binds The People Together

257. John Mix Stanley, *Portraits of North American Indians,* Smithsonian Institution, "Miscellaneous Collections," 1852, vol. II, p. 19, Washington, D.C.
258. Walter McClintock, *Old Indian Trails* (Boston: Houghton Mifflin Co., 1923), p. 303.
259. Ahenakew, *op. cit.,* p. 75.
260. Kennedy, *The Assiniboines, op. cit.,* p. 60.
261. Standing Bear, *Land of the Spotted Eagle, op. cit.,* p. 129.
262. Brown, *Voices of Earth and Sky, op. cit.,* p. 85.
263. Joseph S. Karol, ed., *Red Horse Owner's Winter Count* (Martin, South Dakota: Booster Publishing Co., 1969), p. 5.
264. Ball, *op. cit.,* p. 104.
265. Chief Eagle, *op. cit.,* p. 145.
266. Goodwin, *op. cit.,* p. XV.
267. Gerald Vizenor, *The Everlasting Sky: New Voices from the Chippewa* (New York: Crowell-Collier Press, 1972), p. 69.
268. Kennedy, *Recollections of an Assiniboine Chief, op. cit.,* p. 99.
269. Marquis, *op. cit.,* pp. 383-384.
270. Standing Bear, *Land of the Spotted Eagle, op. cit.,* p. 69.
271. John Fire/Lame Deer, *op. cit.,* p. 45.
272. Barrett, *op. cit.,* p. 77.
273. Sandoz, *These Were the Sioux, op. cit.,* p. 94.
274. William H. Goode, *Outposts of Zion,* 1863, cited in Grant Foreman, *Advancing the Frontier 1830-1860* (Norman: University of Oklahoma Press, 1933), p. 209.
275. Drake, *The Aborig··· al Races of North American, op. cit.,* p. 632.
276. Matthews, *op. cit.,* p. 237 note 157.

277. Joseph Cash and Herbert Hoover, eds., *To Be An Indian* (New York: Holt, Rinehart & Winston, 1971), p. 28.

278. Storm, *op. cit.*, p. 243.

The Human Race: The Circle Unites The People As One Nation

279. John Fire/Lame Deer, *op. cit.*, pp. 265-266.

280. *American Indian Magazine*, Quarterly Journal of the Society of American Indians, vol. 4, no. 2 (1916).

281. Benjamin Franklin, *A Treaty of Friendship held with the Chiefs of the Six Nations at Philadelphia, in September and October, 1736*, Philadelphia: Benjamin Franklin, 1737, reprinted in Julian P. Boyd, ed., *Indian Treaties Printed by Benjamin Franklin, 1736-1762* (Philadelphia: Historical Society of Pennsylvania, 1938), p. 7.

282. Lucy Kramer Cohen, ed, *The Legal Conscience: Selected Papers of Felix S. Cohen* (New Haven: Yale University Press, 1960), pp. 315-316.

283. W. Fletcher Johnson, *Life of Sitting Bull and History of the Indian War of 1890-91* (No City: Edgewood Publishing Co., 1891), p. 155.

284. *Washington Evening Star*, 5 and 7 February 1891.

285. United States, *Senate Document #88, op. cit.*, p. 202.

286. Qoyawayma, *op. cit.*, p. 101.

287. Philippe de Trobriand, *Vie Militaire Dans Le Dakota, Notes Et Souvenirs (1867-1869)*, trans. George Francis Will, *Army Life in Dakota*, Lakeside Classics series, no. 39 (Chicago: R. R. Donnelley & Sons Co., 1941), p. 82.

288. Drake, *The Aboriginal Races of North America, op. cit.*, p. 632.

289. Fletcher, *The Omaha Tribe*, Bison Book, 1972, *op. cit.*, p. 394.

290. McKenney, *op. cit.*, p. 321.

291. Drake, *The Aboriginal Races of North America, op. cit.*, pp. 562-563.

292. Drake, *The Aboriginal Races of North America, op. cit.*, pp. 390-391.

293. Louis Thomas Jones, *Aboriginal American Oratory: The Tradition of Eloquence Among the Indians of the United States* (Los Angeles: Southwest Museum, 1965), p. 118.

294. *Red Cloud Country*, "The Death of Crazy Horse: His Last Words," vol. 14, no. 3 (1977), Red Cloud Indian School (Holy Rosary Mission), Pine Ridge, South Dakota.

295. Drake, *The Aboriginal Races of North America, op. cit.*, p. 43.

296. Eugene Current-Garcia, ed., with Dorothy B. Hatfield, *Shem, Ham, and Japheth; The Papers of W. O. Tuggle* (Athens, Georgia: University of Georgia Press, 1973), p. 148.

297. Samuel G. Goodrich, *Lives of Celebrated American Indians* (Boston: Bradbury, Soden & Co., 1843), p. 179.

298. Drake, *The Aboriginal Races of North America, op. cit.*, p. 619.

299. Bemis, *op. cit.*, n.p.

300. Drake, *The Aboriginal Races of North America, op. cit.*, p. 527.

301. Drake, *The Aboriginal Races of North America, op. cit.*, pp. 635-636.

302. Drake, *The Aboriginal Races of North America, op. cit.*, p. 450.

303. Drake, *The Aboriginal Races of North America, op. cit.*, pp. 617-618.

304. James Mooney, *Calendar History of the Kiowa Indians*, Bureau of American Ethnology, 17th annual report, part 1, 1895-1896 (Washington: Government Printing Office, 1897), p. 208.

305. Sun Bear, *op. cit.*, p. 6.

306. Eastman, *The Indian Today, op. cit.*, pp. 149-150.

307. Fletcher, *The Hako: a Pawnee Ceremony, op. cit.*, p. 15.

308. Henry R. Schoolcraft, *History of the Indian Tribes of the United States: ... their Ancient Status*, published by order of Congress, vol. 6 (Philadelphia: J. B. Lippincott & Co., 1857), p. 507.

309. Burton, *op. cit.*, p. 25.

310. Alford, *op. cit.*, p. 167.

311. Indian Springs State Park, Indian Springs, Georgia, brochure, cited in Jesse Burt and Robert B. Ferguson, *Indians of the Southeast: Then and Now* (Nashville: Abingdon Press, 1973), p. 174.

312. W. Fletcher Johnson, *op. cit.* p. 201.

313. C. Fayne Porter, *Our Indian Heritage: Profiles of 12 Great Leaders* (Philadelphia: Chilton Book Co., 1964), p. 142.

314. Steiger, *op. cit.*, pp. 106-107.

315. Drake, *The Aboriginal Races of North America, op. cit.*, p. 41.

316. Peter Farb, *Man's Rise to Civilization as Shown by the Indians of North America* (New York: E. P. Dutton & Co., 1968), p. 292.

317. Drake, *The Aboriginal Races of North America, op. cit.*, p. 386.

318. Porter, *op. cit.*, p. 141.

319. John Fire/Lame Deer, *op. cit.*, p. 18.

320. Sun Bear, *op. cit.*, p. 29.

321. George E. Hyde, *Spotted Tail's Folk: A History of the Brulé Sioux*, Civilization of the American Indian series, no. 57 (Norman: University of Oklahoma Press, 1961), p. 247.

322. Cadwallader Colden, *The History of the Five Indian Nations of Canada*, London, 1747, reprint New York: New Amsterdam Book Company, 1902, cited in Wilcomb E. Washburn, ed., *The Indian and the White Man*, documents in American Civilization series (Garden City, New York: Doubleday & Company, Inc., Anchor Books, 1964), p. 332.

323. John E. Weems, *Death Song: the last of the Indian Wars* (Garden City, New York: Doubleday & Company, Inc., 1976), p. 271.

324. Drake, *The Aboriginal Races of North America, op. cit.*, pp. 598-599.

325. Eastman, *The Soul of the Indian, op. cit.*, pp. 9-11.

326. M. I. McCreight, *Firewater and Forked Tongues* (Pasadena: Trails End Publishing Co., 1947), p. 61.

327. Steiner, *op. cit.*, p. 106.

328. Vestal, *op. cit.*, p. 244.

329. *An Uncommon Controversy, op. cit.* p. 29.

Bibliography

Ahenakew, Edward. *Voices of the Plains Cree.* Edited by Ruth M. Bush. Toronto: McClelland & Stewart Limited, 1973.

Bad Heart Bull, Amos. *A Pictographic History of the Oglala Sioux.* Lincoln: University of Nebraska, 1967.

Barrows, William. *The Indian's Side of the Indian Question.* Boston: D. Lothrop Co., 1888.

Beverley, Robert. *The History and Present State of Virginia.* London: R. Parker, 1705, revised 1722.

Bradford, William. *Of Plymouth Plantation, 1620-1647.* Boston, 1856. Edited by Samuel Eliot Morison. New York: Modern Library, 1967.

Brandt, Richard S. *Hopi Ethics.* Chicago: University of Chicago Press, 1954.

Brinton, Daniel G. *Ancient Nahuatl Poetry.* Library of American Literature, vol. 7. Philadelphia, 1887.

Brinton, Daniel G. "The Books of Chilam Balam." In *Essays of an Americanist.* Philadelphia, 1890.

Butcher, Devereux. *Exploring Our Prehistoric Indian Ruins.* Washington: National Parks Association, 1960.

Catlin, George. *Letters and Notes.* . . . 1841. Reprint. Minneapolis: Ross & Haines, 1965.

Colden, Cadwallader. *History of the Five Nations Depending on the Province of New-York in America.* Ithaca, New York: Cornell University Press, Great Seal Books, 1958.

Cornplanter, Jesse J. *Legends of the Longhouse.* Port Washington, New York: Ira J. Friedman, 1963.

Crocchiola, Stanley F. H. *Satanta and the Kiowas.* Borger, Texas: Hess, 1968.

Cushing, Frank Hamilton. *Outlines of Zuñi Creation Myths.* Bureau of American Ethnology, 13th annual report, 1891-1892. Washington: Government Printing Office, 1896.

Drake, Samuel G. *The Aboriginal Races of North America.* Revised J. W. O'Neill, 15th edition. Philadelphia: Charles Desilver, 1860.

Evarts, Jeremiah. *Speeches on the Passage of the Bill for the Removal of the Indians.* Boston: Perkins & Marvin, 1830.

Flannery, Regina. *An Analysis of Coastal Algonquian Culture.* Anthropological series, no. 7. Washington: Catholic University of America, 1939.

Fletcher, Alice C. *The Hako: A Pawnee Ceremony.* Bureau of American Ethnology, 22nd annual report, part 2, 1900-1901. Washington: Government Printing Office, 1904.

Fletcher, Alice C.; Francis LaFlesche. *The Omaha Tribe.* Bureau of American Ethnology, 27th annual report, 1905-1906. Washington: Government Printing Office, 1911.

Franklin, Benjamin. *A Narrative of the Late Massacres . . . With Observations on the Same.* Philadelphia, 1764. *The Papers of Benjamin Franklin.* Volume 11. Edited by Leonard W. Labaree. New Haven: Yale University Press, 1967.

Hagan, William T. *The Indian in American History.* Publication no. 50. Service Center for Teachers of History, American Historical Association. New York: The Macmillan Co., 1963. Revised 1971.

Harmon, George D. *Sixty Years of Indian Affairs, Political, Economic, and Diplomatic, 1789-1850.* Chapel Hill: University of North Carolina Press, 1941.

Heckewelder, John G. *An Account of the History, Manners, and Customs of the Indian Nations. . . .* Philadelphia, 1819. Edited by Rev. William C. Reichel. Memoirs of the Historical Society of Pennsylvania. Philadelphia, 1876.

Hennepin, Louis. *A New Discovery of a Vast Country in America. . . .* 1698. Edited by Reuben Gold Thwaites. Reprint, 2 vols. Chicago: A. C. McClurg & Co., 1903.

Hodge, Frederick W., ed. *Handbook of American Indians North of Mexico.* Bureau of American Ethnology, bulletin no. 30, parts 1 and 2, 1907-1910. Washington: Government Printing Office, reprint, 1912.

Jackson, Helen Hunt. *A Century of Dishonor.* 1885. Revised. Boston: Little, Brown, & Co., 1909.

Jefferson, Thomas. *Notes on the State of Virginia. . . .* 1785. Edited by William Peden. Chapel Hill: University of North Carolina Press, 1955.

Kennedy, Dan (Ochankugahe). *Recollections of an Assiniboine Chief.* Edited by James R. Stevens. Toronto: McClelland & Stewart Limited, 1972.

Kennedy, Michael, ed. *The Assiniboines, From the Accounts of the Old Ones, Told to First Boy (James Larpenteur Long).* Originally published as *Land of Nakoda, The Assiniboines.* 1942. New edition. Civilization of the American Indian series, no. 58. Norman: University of Oklahoma Press, 1961.

Lahontan, Louis A., Baron de. *New Voyages to North America.* 1703. Edited by Reuben Gold Thwaites. Chicago: A. C. McClurg & Co., 2 vols., 1905.

Lame Deer (John Fire); Richard Erdoes. *Lame Deer, Seeker of Visions.* New York: Simon & Schuster, Touchstone Books, 1972.

Leckie, William H. *The Buffalo Soldiers.* Norman: University of Oklahoma Press, 1967.

Linderman, Frank B. *Plenty-coups, Chief of the Crows.* Lincoln: University of Nebraska Press, 1930, 1957.

MacGowan, Kenneth; Joseph A. Hester, Jr. *Early Man in the New World.* Garden City, New York: Doubleday-Anchor, 1962.

McNickle, D'Arcy. *They Came Here First.* Philadelphia: J. B. Lippincott, 1949.

Martineau, LaVan. *The Rocks Begin to Speak.* Las Vegas, Nevada: KC Publications, 1973.

Meyer, Roy W. *History of the Santee Sioux.* Lincoln: University of Nebraska Press, 1967.

Mooney, James. *Siouan Tribes of the East.* Bureau of American Ethnology, bulletin 22. Washington: Government Printing Office, 1894.

Nelson, Nels Christian. *The Antiquity of Man in America in the Light of Archeology.* Smithsonian Institution, annual report, 1935. Washington: Government Printing Office, 1936.

Newcomb, William W., Jr. *The Culture and Acculturation of the Delaware Indians.* Museum of Anthropology, Anthropological Papers, no. 10. Ann Arbor: University of Michigan Press, 1956.

Ortiz, Alfonso. *The Tewa World: Space, Time, Being, and Becoming in a Pueblo Society*. Chicago: University of Chicago Press, 1969.

Parker, Arthur C. *A History of the Seneca Indians*. Empire State Historical Publication, no. 43. 1926. Port Washington, New York: Ira J. Friedman, 1967.

Qoyawayma, Polingaysi. *No Turning Back*. As told to Vada F. Carlson. Albuquerque: University of New Mexico Press, 1964.

Quimby, George I. *Indian Life in the Upper Great Lakes: 11,000 B.C. to A.D. 1800*. Chicago: University of Chicago Press, 1960.

Royce, Charles C. *The Cherokee Nation of Indians*. Bureau of American Ethnology, 5th annual report, 1883-1884. Washington: Government Printing Office, 1887.

Sandoz, Mari. *These Were the Sioux*. New York: Hastings House Publishers, 1961.

Smith, John. *Works, 1608-1631*. Edited by Edward Arber. Birmingham, England, 1884, 2 vols. Revised by A. G. Bradley. Edinburgh: John Grant, 1910.

Spicer, E. H. *Pascua, A Yaqui Village in Arizona*. Chicago: University of Chicago Press, 1940.

Standing Bear, Luther. *Land of the Spotted Eagle*. Boston: Houghton-Mifflin Co., 1933.

Steiger, Brad. *Medicine Talk*. New York: Doubleday & Co., 1975.

Stevenson, James. *Ceremonial of Hasjelti Dailjis*. Bureau of American Ethnology, 8th annual report, 1886-1887. Washington: Government Printing Office, 1891.

Storm, Hyemeyohsts. *Seven Arrows*. New York: Harper & Row Publishers, 1972.

Thatcher, Benjamin B. *Tales of the Indians ... from Authentic Sources*. Boston: Waitt and Dow, 1831.

Thrapp, Dan L. *The Conquest of Apacheria*. Norman: University of Oklahoma Press, 1967.

Thwaites, Reuben Gold, ed. *The Jesuit Relations and Allied Documents: Travels and Explorations of the Jesuit Missionaries in New France, 1619-1791....* 73 vols. Cleveland: Burrows Brothers, 1900.

Turner, Katherine C. *Red Men Calling on the Great White Father*. Norman: University of Oklahoma Press, 1951.

Tyler, Lyon Gardiner, ed. *Narratives of Early Virginia 1606-1625*. Original Narratives of Early American History series. New York: Charles Scribner's Sons, 1907.

United States, Congress, "Massacre of the Cheyenne Indians," in *Report of the Joint Committee on the Conduct of the War*, 38th Congress, 2nd session, 1865.

Vestal, Stanley. *New Sources of Indian History 1850-91*. Norman: University of Oklahoma Press, 1934.

Ware, Eugene F. *The Indian War of 1864*. Topeka, Kansas: Crane & Co., 1911.

Crows by Frank B. Linderman. Copyright 1930, 1957. Reprinted by permission of Sarah J. Hatfield, Trustee.

FOOTNOTES 50, 58, 107, 305, 320. From *Buffalo Hearts* by Sun Bear. Copyright © 1970 by Sun Bear. By permission of Sun Bear, Bear Tribe Publishing, P. O. Box 9167, Spokane, Washington 99209.

FOOTNOTES 51, 55, 56, 72, 85, 100, 109, 220, 228, 259. From *Voices of the Plains Cree* by Edward Ahenakew. Reprinted by permission of The Canadian Publishers, McClelland and Stewart Limited, Toronto.

FOOTNOTES 52, 99, 252, 310. From *Civilization* by Thomas Wildcat Alford. Copyright © by University of Oklahoma Press. Reprinted by permission of University of Oklahoma Press.

FOOTNOTES 62, 123, 193. From *Sun Chief: The Autobiography of a Hopi Indian* edited by Leo W. Simmons. Copyright 1942, 1967. Reprinted by permission of Yale University Press.

FOOTNOTES 63, 157, 183, 204, 213, 230, 238, 246, 247, 273. From *These Were the Sioux.* Copyright © 1961 by Mari Sandoz. By permission of Hastings House, Publishers.

FOOTNOTES 74, 169, 225, 235, 266. From *The Social Organization of the Western Apache* by Grenville Goodwin. Copyright © 1942 by Grenville Goodwin. By permission of University of Chicago Press.

FOOTNOTES 79, 90, 152, 202, 254, 268. From *Recollections of an Assiniboine Chief* by Dan Kennedy. Reprinted by permission of the Canadian Publishers, McClelland and Stewart Limited, Toronto.

FOOTNOTES 88, 137, 156, 328. From *Sitting Bull, Champion of the Sioux* by Stanley Vestal. Civilization of the American Indian series #46. Copyright © 1932 by Houghton Mifflin Co. and 1957 by University of Oklahoma Press. Reprinted by permission of University of Oklahoma Press.

FOOTNOTES 96, 178. From *Two Leggings* by Peter Nabokov (T. Y. Crowell). Copyright © 1967 by Peter Nabokov. Reprinted by permission of Harper & Row, Publishers, Inc.

FOOTNOTES 105, 264. By permission from *In the Days of Victorio,* James Kaywakla, Narrator, by Eve Ball, Tucson: University of Arizona Press, copyright 1970.

FOOTNOTES 111, 215. By permission from *A Pima Remembers,* George Webb, Tucson: University of Arizona Press, copyright 1959.

FOOTNOTE 117. From *Book of the Eskimos* by Peter Freuchen. Copyright © 1961 by Dagmar Freuchen. Reprinted by permission of the Harold Matson Company, Inc.

FOOTNOTES 122, 124, 309. From *Indian Heritage, Indian Pride* by Jimalee Burton (Ho-chee-nee). Copyright © 1974 by University of Oklahoma Press. Reprinted by permission of University of Oklahoma Press.

FOOTNOTES 129, 217. From *The Navaho* by Clyde Kluckhohn and Dorothea

Index